Jama

Everything You Need to Know

Copyright © 2023 by Noah Gil-Smith.
All rights reserved. No part of this book may be reproduced, distributed, or transmitted in any form or by any means, including photocopying, recording, or other electronic or mechanical methods, without the prior written permission of the publisher, except in the case of brief quotations embodied in critical reviews and certain other noncommercial uses permitted by copyright law. This book was created with the assistance of Artificial Intelligence. The content presented in this book is for entertainment purposes only. It should not be considered as a substitute for professional advice or comprehensive research. Readers are encouraged to independently verify any information and consult relevant experts for specific matters. The author and publisher disclaim any liability or responsibility for any loss, injury, or inconvenience caused or alleged to be caused directly or indirectly by the information presented in this book.

Introduction: Discovering Jamaica's Vibrant Spirit 6

A Glimpse of Jamaica's Rich History 8

The Indigenous Roots: Arawak and Taino Influence 10

The Arrival of the Europeans: Colonial Era Beginnings 12

The Maroons: Defenders of Freedom and Identity 14

From Plantations to Independence: Jamaica's Struggle for Freedom 16

Modern Jamaica: The Journey to Nationhood 18

The Enchanting Wildlife of Jamaica 20

A Taste of Paradise: Jamaican Cuisine Unveiled 22

Ackee and Saltfish: The National Dish and Beyond 24

Jamaican Jerk: A Fiery Culinary Delight 26

Satisfying Your Sweet Tooth: Jamaican Desserts 28

Delving into Jamaican Fruits and Tropical Delicacies 30

Exploring Jamaica's Iconic Tourist Sights 32

Negril's White Sands and Turquoise Waters 34

Ocho Rios: Waterfalls and Beyond 36

The Majesty of the Blue Mountains 38

The Enigmatic Luminous Lagoon: Nature's Light Show 40

Kingston: The Capital of Culture and Heritage 42

Montego Bay: Jamaica's Gateway to the World 44

Port Antonio: A Hidden Gem in the Caribbean 46

Spanish Town: Tracing Jamaica's Colonial Past 48

Falmouth: A Historic Georgian Gem 50

The Vibrant Rastafarian Culture of Jamaica 52

Reggae Music: Bob Marley's Legacy and Beyond 54

Dancehall: The Rhythmic Heartbeat of Jamaica 56

Junkanoo: A Festive Celebration of African Roots 58

Embracing the Laid-Back Lifestyle of Jamaica 60

Festivals and Celebrations: Joyous Jamaican Traditions 62

The Influence of Religion in Jamaican Culture 64

Art and Craftsmanship: Expressions of Jamaican Creativity 66

Literature and Poetry: The Written Soul of Jamaica 68

Patois: The Colorful Language of the Island 70

Jamaican English: Understanding the Linguistic Blend 72

Exploring Jamaican Folklore and Superstitions 74

The Impact of Sports on Jamaican Identity 76

Jamaica's Love for Cricket and Athletic Glory 78

Healing Traditions: Jamaican Medicinal Practices 80

Ecotourism in Jamaica: Preserving Paradise 82

Jamaica's Unique Blend of Modern and Traditional Architecture 84

Sustainability and Environmental Challenges in Jamaica 86

Jamaican Economy: From Agriculture to Tourism 88

Education and Literacy in Jamaica 90

Social Issues and Challenges Faced by the Nation 92

Epilogue 94

Introduction: Discovering Jamaica's Vibrant Spirit

Welcome to the breathtaking island of Jamaica, a land where vibrant colors, rhythmic beats, and warm smiles beckon you to explore its rich tapestry of history, culture, and natural wonders. Nestled in the heart of the Caribbean, Jamaica is a paradise that has captivated the hearts of travelers and adventurers for centuries.

As you set foot on this enchanting island, you'll immediately sense the infectious spirit that permeates its very essence. From the moment the sun rises over the misty Blue Mountains to the lively beat of reggae music that echoes through the streets, Jamaica exudes an energy that is both intoxicating and invigorating.

Jamaica's history is a fascinating blend of indigenous roots, colonial influence, and the resilient spirit of its people. Before the arrival of European explorers, the Arawak and Taino peoples thrived on the island, leaving behind a legacy of art, agriculture, and spirituality that continues to shape Jamaican culture to this day.

With the arrival of the Spanish in the 15th century, Jamaica's fate took a turn, as it became a coveted prize in the race for dominance among European powers. It wasn't until the British took control in the mid-17th century that the island's plantation economy flourished, with sugarcane becoming the driving force behind the transatlantic slave trade.

Yet, amidst the struggles and hardships faced by the enslaved, a powerful force for freedom emerged in the form of the Maroons. These brave and resourceful communities fought for their independence, leading to the signing of peace treaties with the British and establishing autonomous regions in the rugged interior.

Jamaica's path to independence was marked by determination and vision. On August 6, 1962, the nation proudly unfurled its own flag, signaling a new era of self-governance. Since then, the Jamaican people have continuously shaped their destiny, embracing their heritage while carving out a place in the modern world.

But Jamaica is much more than just a collection of historical events. It's a living, breathing testament to the colorful fusion of cultures and traditions that have influenced its identity. The warmth of the Jamaican people, known for their genuine hospitality, radiates through every interaction, making visitors feel like old friends.

The island's diverse landscape is a testament to Mother Nature's artistic prowess. From the stunning beaches of Negril and Montego Bay to the lush rainforests of Cockpit Country and the majestic cliffs of the South Coast, Jamaica's natural beauty is a sight to behold.

No exploration of Jamaica would be complete without indulging in its mouthwatering cuisine. The blend of African, European, and Indigenous flavors creates a unique culinary experience. From the savory delights of jerk chicken and pork to the iconic national dish, ackee and saltfish, every bite tells a story of the island's history.

Jamaica's rich musical heritage is equally captivating. Reggae, with its soulful rhythms and meaningful lyrics, has become a global phenomenon thanks to legendary artists like Bob Marley, who used his music to champion peace, love, and social justice.

As you immerse yourself in Jamaica's vibrant spirit, you'll encounter a tapestry of festivals and celebrations that reflect the nation's colorful soul. From the exuberant Junkanoo parades to the somber yet soul-stirring rituals of the Kumina, each event is a kaleidoscope of emotions that captures the essence of Jamaican life.

Join us as we embark on this journey through Jamaica's past, present, and future. Together, we'll unveil the hidden treasures and unveil the captivating stories that have shaped this remarkable island. Whether you're a first-time visitor or a seasoned traveler, Jamaica's vibrant spirit will undoubtedly leave an indelible mark on your heart and soul. So, fasten your seatbelt, embrace the rhythm of the island, and let the adventure begin!

A Glimpse of Jamaica's Rich History

Jamaica's history is a tapestry woven with threads of indigenous cultures, European colonization, slavery, emancipation, and the triumphant struggle for independence. Situated in the Caribbean Sea, this island nation has been a coveted jewel sought after by various colonial powers due to its strategic location and abundant resources.

Long before European explorers set foot on its shores, the Arawak and Taino peoples inhabited Jamaica. These indigenous communities lived in harmony with nature, engaging in agriculture, fishing, and crafting intricate art that reflected their spiritual beliefs. Their existence on the island dates back to at least 600 AD, and their legacy continues to influence Jamaican culture and traditions today.

In 1494, Christopher Columbus arrived in Jamaica during his second voyage to the New World, claiming the island for Spain. The Spanish influence on Jamaica was significant, but colonization was not without conflict. The indigenous population faced disease, enslavement, and forced labor under the Spanish rule, leading to a drastic decline in their numbers.

By the mid-17th century, the British, led by Sir William Penn and General Robert Venables, wrested control of Jamaica from the Spanish, making it an English colony. With the island's fertile soil and suitable climate, the plantation system flourished, centered around the cultivation of sugarcane. To meet the demand for labor, the transatlantic slave trade was brutally intensified, with millions of Africans forcibly brought to Jamaica and other Caribbean colonies.

The enslaved Africans endured unimaginable suffering, yet their resilience and indomitable spirit laid the foundation for Jamaican culture as it exists today. They retained and adapted elements of their African heritage, incorporating them into music, dance, art, and religious practices, creating a unique cultural amalgamation that defines Jamaica's identity.

The 18th century brought about significant changes to the island's social fabric. The Maroons, descendants of escaped slaves who formed autonomous communities in the mountainous regions, actively resisted British authority. They waged wars against the colonial forces, ultimately leading to peace treaties that granted them freedom and self-governance.

As the winds of change swept through the Caribbean, so did the ideas of freedom and equality. The 19th century witnessed the rise of abolitionist movements, and the efforts of individuals like William Knibb and Mary Seacole contributed to the cause of ending slavery. Finally, in 1834, the British Parliament passed the Emancipation Act, officially abolishing slavery in Jamaica.

The post-emancipation era brought its own set of challenges. With the end of slavery, many former slaves sought better opportunities and independence, leading to the emergence of small-scale agriculture and the establishment of free villages. Jamaican society began to take shape, laying the groundwork for the nation's future.

Throughout the 20th century, Jamaica experienced a series of social, political, and cultural transformations. The island saw the rise of influential political leaders, including Norman Manley and Alexander Bustamante, who played pivotal roles in the country's quest for self-governance. On August 6, 1962, Jamaica proudly gained independence from British rule, becoming a sovereign nation within the Commonwealth.

Independence brought with it new challenges and opportunities. Jamaica's journey towards economic and social progress has been characterized by a dynamic blend of successes and setbacks. The country has grappled with issues such as crime, economic inequality, and environmental concerns, but its people have shown remarkable resilience and determination in overcoming these hurdles.

Today, Jamaica stands as a proud nation with a rich history and a vibrant culture that continues to captivate the world. Its people embrace their heritage while embracing modernity, and the island's beauty, music, cuisine, and warm hospitality attract visitors from all corners of the globe.

The Indigenous Roots: Arawak and Taino Influence

In the lush landscapes of Jamaica, long before the arrival of European explorers, thriving indigenous communities known as the Arawak and Taino peoples called the island home. These ancient inhabitants had a profound influence on the island's culture, lifestyle, and traditions, leaving an indelible mark on Jamaica's history that resonates even today.

The Arawak and Taino civilizations were part of the larger Arawakan language family that inhabited various islands across the Caribbean. Their arrival in Jamaica is estimated to have occurred around 600 AD, and they quickly adapted to the island's diverse environments, utilizing the land's resources for sustenance and prosperity.

Living in close harmony with nature, the Arawak and Taino were skilled agriculturalists. They cultivated crops like cassava, maize, sweet potatoes, and yams, demonstrating a deep understanding of the land's fertility and its potential for sustaining their communities. These agricultural practices not only provided them with nourishment but also formed the foundation of their vibrant culture.

The Arawak and Taino societies were organized into chiefdoms, with each community led by a chief or cacique. Social structures were well-defined, and everyone had a role to play in maintaining the cohesion and stability of the community. Their hierarchical system promoted cooperation and collective decision-making, ensuring that the needs of all members were met.

Both cultures were renowned for their impressive craftsmanship and artistic expression. They created exquisite pottery, weaving, and intricate artwork, depicting scenes from their daily lives and their spiritual beliefs. These artifacts not only served utilitarian purposes but also carried immense cultural significance, reflecting their reverence for nature and spirituality.

The Arawak and Taino peoples also held strong spiritual beliefs, attributing sacred significance to natural elements such as the sun, moon, and stars. They practiced polytheism, worshipping a pantheon of deities and spirits. Their spirituality was deeply intertwined with their daily activities, and rituals played a crucial role in marking important life events and agricultural cycles.

A crucial aspect of their cultural heritage was the art of storytelling. Through oral traditions, they passed down their history, myths, legends, and ancestral wisdom from one generation to another. These narratives provided a foundation for their identity and fostered a sense of unity among their people, transcending time and preserving their legacy.

Interaction with other Caribbean cultures and trade networks enriched their lives. Through these connections, they acquired items such as pottery, tools, and jewelry that showcased their trade prowess and interconnectedness with neighboring communities.

With the arrival of Christopher Columbus and subsequent European explorers, the lives of the Arawak and Taino peoples took an irrevocable turn. The introduction of foreign diseases and the harsh treatment imposed by the colonizers resulted in a tragic decline in their population. Their communities, once thriving and vibrant, faced devastating challenges, leading to the gradual disappearance of their cultures and traditions.

Despite the profound impact of European colonization, the Arawak and Taino influence continues to resonate in the hearts of the Jamaican people. Efforts to preserve and revive elements of their heritage persist, as archaeologists, historians, and local communities work together to uncover the remnants of this ancient past.

The Arrival of the Europeans: Colonial Era Beginnings

As the sun set on the 14th of May in 1494, an expedition led by Christopher Columbus sighted the shores of an enchanting island in the Caribbean Sea. Little did he know that this discovery marked the beginning of a new era that would forever alter the course of history for the island now known as Jamaica.

The arrival of the Europeans on Jamaican soil brought with it a wave of curiosity, ambition, and the desire to claim new territories in the name of their respective monarchs. For Columbus and his crew, Jamaica presented a potential haven for resources, wealth, and strategic advantage in the exploration of the New World.

Spain, seeking to expand its dominion over the newfound lands, wasted no time in asserting its control over Jamaica. By the early 1500s, Spanish settlements began to take root along the coast, with Port Royal becoming a significant center of commerce and administration. The Spanish Crown saw Jamaica as a valuable outpost for its lucrative trade in gold, silver, and other valuable commodities.

The indigenous Arawak and Taino peoples, who had inhabited the island for centuries, encountered the Europeans with a mix of curiosity and trepidation. The initial interactions were relatively peaceful, but the ambitions of the newcomers would soon set a darker course for Jamaica's history.

As the Spanish foothold on the island solidified, the Arawak and Taino communities faced the devastating consequences of European contact. Foreign diseases brought by the Europeans wreaked havoc on their populations, leading to a tragic decline in numbers. The colonizers' demand for labor in the growing sugar cane plantations resulted in forced labor and enslavement of the indigenous peoples.

Amidst the struggles faced by the indigenous population, the Spanish settlers established haciendas and encomiendas, vast agricultural estates that exploited both indigenous labor and imported African slaves. The growing wealth of the colonizers came at a high cost to the original inhabitants, who endured hardships and subjugation under the weight of colonial rule.

The Spanish rule over Jamaica was not without resistance. The indigenous peoples, facing the brutality of their oppressors, sometimes revolted against the colonial authority. However, the might of the Spanish forces proved overwhelming, quelling these uprisings and solidifying their control over the island.

As the 17th century approached, the allure of Jamaica continued to attract European powers vying for dominance in the Caribbean. In 1655, the English, under the command of Admiral William Penn and General Robert Venables, successfully captured Jamaica from the weakened Spanish forces. This marked the end of Spanish rule on the island and the beginning of a new chapter in Jamaica's colonial history.

Under British rule, Jamaica saw a shift in economic priorities. The fertile lands of the island were ideal for sugar cane cultivation, and the plantation system expanded rapidly. The British, much like the Spanish before them, relied on enslaved Africans to toil on the plantations, forging a brutal and exploitative system that extracted wealth from the toil and suffering of countless individuals.

As the British influence deepened, the demography of Jamaica transformed drastically. The African population grew significantly due to the continued importation of slaves, laying the foundation for the diverse cultural mosaic that characterizes Jamaica today.

Despite the oppressive nature of colonial rule, the blending of diverse cultures began to take shape. Enslaved Africans infused their rich traditions, languages, music, and religious practices into the fabric of Jamaican society. This fusion of cultures, known as creolization, laid the groundwork for the vibrant and unique Jamaican culture that would emerge in the centuries to come.

The colonial era was marked by both hardship and resilience, as the Arawak and Taino peoples endured the impact of European colonization, while enslaved Africans retained their cultural identities amidst unimaginable adversity.

The Maroons: Defenders of Freedom and Identity

In the heart of Jamaica's rugged terrain and dense forests, a story of resistance, courage, and indomitable spirit unfolds with the rise of the Maroons. The Maroons were communities of escaped African slaves who sought refuge and fought for their freedom against the oppressive forces of European colonization. Their legacy as defenders of freedom and identity remains an integral part of Jamaica's history.

The term "Maroon" is believed to have originated from the Spanish word "cimarrón," meaning wild or untamed. As the 17th century brought the expansion of the plantation economy, life for the enslaved Africans on the sugar and coffee estates of Jamaica became unbearable. Forced labor, brutal treatment, and inhumane living conditions compelled many enslaved individuals to seek escape.

Fleeing from the plantations, these brave souls sought sanctuary in the island's rugged interior. There, amidst the dense forests and mountainous terrain, the Maroon communities were born. Led by courageous individuals, the Maroons established their villages, where they could live freely and govern themselves beyond the reach of the colonial authorities.

The Maroons' resistance to the colonial forces was formidable. Armed with knowledge of the terrain and skilled in guerrilla warfare, they proved to be formidable adversaries for the well-equipped British troops. The Maroons' intimate understanding of the land enabled them to launch ambushes and hit-and-run tactics, allowing them to outmaneuver the colonial forces.

Over time, the Maroons' reputation as skilled warriors grew, as they not only defended their communities but also liberated other enslaved individuals seeking refuge with them. The fight for freedom and resistance against oppression became the foundation of their identity, uniting them in a common cause that transcended tribal and linguistic differences among their diverse African origins.

One of the most significant Maroon leaders in Jamaican history was Nanny of the Maroons. Revered as a legendary figure, Nanny was a strategic and charismatic leader who played a pivotal role in the struggle for freedom. She led the Windward Maroons and was known for her astute military tactics, earning her the nickname "Nanny the Maroon Warrior Queen."

The British colonial authorities recognized the Maroons' formidable resistance and sought to suppress their movements. In 1739, after a series of intense conflicts, a peace treaty known as the Treaty of Cudjoe was signed between the British and the Windward Maroons. This agreement recognized the Maroons' right to live in their communities and govern themselves, thus establishing their autonomy and semi-independent status.

In the years that followed, other Maroon communities also negotiated treaties with the British, further solidifying their freedoms and ensuring the preservation of their cultural heritage. These treaties created a delicate balance between the Maroons and the colonial authorities, shaping the future relationship between the two groups.

The Maroon communities thrived within their territories, developing unique cultural expressions that blended their African heritage with influences from their interactions with the indigenous peoples and the colonial society. Their spiritual beliefs, music, dance, and oral traditions all contributed to the richness of Jamaican culture.

As the abolitionist movement gained momentum in the 19th century, Jamaica saw significant changes in its social and political landscape. Slavery was finally abolished in 1834, granting freedom to thousands of enslaved individuals, but the struggle for equality and civil rights continued.

The legacy of the Maroons lives on, as their descendants and their contributions to Jamaica's history are celebrated and commemorated. Their story is a testament to the human spirit's resilience and determination to resist oppression and claim the right to live freely with dignity and pride.

In modern Jamaica, the Maroons are recognized as a vital part of the nation's heritage. They remain a symbol of the strength and courage of those who fought for freedom and identity against all odds. The Maroons' legacy serves as a powerful reminder of the importance of preserving history and acknowledging the contributions of all those who have shaped the fabric of a nation.

From Plantations to Independence: Jamaica's Struggle for Freedom

As the 19th century dawned, Jamaica stood at a crossroads, its history deeply entwined with the legacy of colonization and the exploitative plantation system. The transition from a slave-based economy to a society striving for independence would be fraught with challenges, resistance, and moments of triumph that would shape the nation's identity for generations to come.

The abolition of slavery in 1834 marked a significant turning point in Jamaica's history. With the emancipation of enslaved individuals, a new era began, albeit one fraught with uncertainty and the struggle for autonomy. The former slaves faced numerous challenges in the post-emancipation period, as they sought to redefine their identities and establish their place in a society that had long dehumanized them.

Though legally freed, the newly emancipated individuals were not granted full freedom. The British colonial authorities introduced a system of apprenticeship, in which former slaves were required to work on the plantations for their former masters for a fixed period, essentially continuing the exploitative labor practices under a different guise. This system bred resentment and discontent among the newly freed population, as it failed to deliver the genuine freedom they had long fought for.

The post-emancipation era also witnessed a wave of social and political movements advocating for change. Baptist and Methodist churches, established during slavery, became centers of community and platforms for social activism. Leaders like Paul Bogle, George William Gordon, and Marcus Garvey emerged as champions of social justice and equality, voicing the grievances of the disenfranchised and advocating for the rights of all Jamaican citizens.

In 1865, a pivotal moment in Jamaica's history occurred with the Morant Bay Rebellion. Led by Paul Bogle, a Baptist deacon, and inspired by the demand for justice and better working conditions, the rebellion was a powerful statement against the oppressive conditions endured by the freed population. The rebellion was met with a violent response from the colonial authorities, resulting in a significant loss of life and a subsequent crackdown on dissent. Nevertheless, the Morant Bay Rebellion served as a catalyst for political change, leading to the establishment of a new governance system that granted Jamaicans greater representation and voice in the decision-making process.

In the early 20th century, Jamaica experienced the rise of Marcus Garvey, a charismatic leader who advocated for black pride, self-determination, and the empowerment of people of African descent worldwide. Garvey's vision of a united and self-reliant black community resonated deeply with Jamaicans and sparked the formation of the Universal Negro Improvement Association (UNIA). Through his powerful speeches and publications, Garvey inspired a sense of pride and unity among Jamaicans, challenging them to embrace their identity and take pride in their cultural heritage.

The struggle for political independence gained momentum in the mid-20th century. In 1944, the People's National Party (PNP) was founded, led by Norman Manley, a prominent attorney and political figure. The PNP advocated for democratic socialism and sought to empower the working class and marginalized communities. Meanwhile, the Jamaican Labour Party (JLP), founded in 1943 and led by Alexander Bustamante, championed the cause of workers' rights and a market-driven economy.

The quest for independence culminated on August 6, 1962, when Jamaica gained its independence from British colonial rule. The nation celebrated this momentous occasion with pride, as it marked the beginning of a new chapter in Jamaican history, with the ability to chart its own course and shape its destiny.

In the decades that followed independence, Jamaica faced various challenges, including economic fluctuations, social inequalities, and political tensions. Nevertheless, the nation's rich cultural heritage, spirited people, and vibrant democracy served as pillars of strength and resilience in navigating these obstacles.

Modern Jamaica: The Journey to Nationhood

As the echoes of independence reverberated across the island on August 6, 1962, Jamaica embarked on a new and transformative journey towards nationhood. The post-independence era would witness the nation's evolution through triumphs, challenges, and moments of self-discovery that would shape its identity in the modern world.

With the departure of British colonial rule, Jamaica faced the task of defining its political and social landscape. The initial years of independence saw the rise of the Jamaica Labour Party (JLP), led by Sir Alexander Bustamante, and the People's National Party (PNP), led by Norman Manley. These two political parties have played a prominent role in shaping the nation's governance since independence.

Sir Alexander Bustamante, known affectionately as "Busta," became Jamaica's first Prime Minister and was instrumental in navigating the nation's early years as a sovereign state. Under his leadership, the country focused on economic development and sought to foster national pride and identity among its people.

Following Bustamante's tenure, his cousin Sir Donald Sangster assumed the role of Prime Minister in 1964. Tragically, Sangster's term was cut short by his untimely death in 1967, marking the first succession of leadership in the young nation's history.

In 1972, the PNP, led by Michael Manley, son of Norman Manley, returned to power. Michael Manley's leadership was characterized by a vision of democratic socialism, seeking to address social inequalities and uplift marginalized communities. During his time in office, Jamaica experienced a period of significant social and economic reforms, including the establishment of free education and land redistribution policies.

The 1970s also saw Jamaica's active engagement in international affairs, with Michael Manley playing a prominent role in the Non-Aligned Movement and advocating for a more equitable global order. However, the economic challenges faced by the nation during this period resulted in increasing debt and strained relationships with international lending institutions.

In the 1980s, the JLP, led by Edward Seaga, regained power, emphasizing market-oriented economic policies and strengthening ties with the United States. Seaga's tenure saw the implementation of economic reforms aimed at stimulating foreign investment and promoting export-oriented industries.

The transition from the 20th to the 21st century marked a period of political and social evolution in Jamaica. The PNP, under the leadership of P.J. Patterson, returned to power in the 1990s, advocating for policies focused on national development, infrastructure improvement, and social welfare programs.

As the nation moved forward, it faced challenges such as crime, economic fluctuations, and social inequalities. Nevertheless, Jamaica's vibrant culture, music, and tourism industry continued to capture the world's imagination and attract visitors from far and wide.

The 21st century brought new opportunities and challenges for Jamaica. The island's natural beauty, along with its rich cultural heritage, continued to be a source of national pride and economic strength through its thriving tourism industry.

Jamaica's journey to nationhood has been one of resilience, determination, and self-discovery. The nation has embraced its past while striving to create a brighter future for its people. Education, healthcare, and economic diversification remain key focuses for the nation as it navigates its path towards sustainable development.

In recent years, Jamaica has seen the emergence of a new generation of leaders, fostering a renewed sense of hope and optimism for the nation's future. Embracing innovation and technology, Jamaica is positioning itself as a competitive player on the global stage, leveraging its unique strengths to foster economic growth and social progress.

The Enchanting Wildlife of Jamaica

Jamaica's lush landscapes and diverse ecosystems offer a haven for an array of enchanting wildlife, making the island a nature lover's paradise. From the majestic birds soaring through the skies to the elusive creatures hiding in the dense rainforests, Jamaica's wildlife is as captivating as it is diverse.

One of the most iconic and celebrated animals of Jamaica is the Doctor Bird, also known as the Swallow Tail Hummingbird (Trochilus polytmus). This exquisite creature is Jamaica's national bird and is famous for its iridescent plumage and unique long tail feathers. The Doctor Bird can be spotted hovering around vibrant tropical flowers, sipping nectar with its specialized brush-tipped tongue.

Jamaica's marine environment is teeming with fascinating sea life. The island is surrounded by coral reefs, providing habitats for an incredible array of fish species. Snorkeling and diving enthusiasts can explore the underwater world and encounter colorful fish like parrotfish, angelfish, and butterflyfish. The reefs are also home to larger inhabitants like moray eels, rays, and even sea turtles.

Venture into the interior of Jamaica, and you'll discover a myriad of intriguing wildlife within the island's rainforests and mountains. The Blue Mountains, with their misty peaks, harbor an array of endemic species found nowhere else on Earth. The Giant Swallowtail Butterfly (Papilio homerus) is one such remarkable creature, with its impressive wingspan making it the largest butterfly in the Western Hemisphere.

The forests are alive with the melodic calls of Jamaican endemic birds, such as the Jamaican Tody (Todus todus) and the Jamaican Woodpecker (Melanerpes radiolatus). These birds add their enchanting songs to the symphony of nature, creating an immersive experience for anyone exploring the wilderness.

Keep a keen eye out for the Jamaican Boa (Epicrates subflavus), a non-venomous snake species endemic to the island. Despite their intimidating reputation, these snakes play a vital role in the ecosystem by controlling rodent populations.

Amidst the trees, you might spot the charismatic Jamaican Fruit Bat (Artibeus jamaicensis) gliding through the twilight hours. These flying mammals are essential pollinators and seed dispersers, contributing to the ecosystem's health.

The enchanting beauty of Jamaica's wildlife is not limited to the land and sea but extends to the freshwater habitats as well. Jamaica's rivers and streams are home to an array of aquatic life, including the Jamaican Coqui (Eleutherodactylus johnstonei), a small tree frog known for its distinctive "ko-kee" call that serenades the nights.

The Jamaican Iguana (Cyclura collei), a critically endangered species, can be found in specific areas of Jamaica, particularly the Hellshire Hills in St. Catherine Parish. Conservation efforts are underway to protect and preserve this magnificent reptile.

Jamaica's wildlife is an integral part of the island's natural heritage and contributes to the nation's rich biodiversity. Efforts to conserve and protect these unique species are of paramount importance in ensuring that future generations can continue to be enchanted by the wonders of Jamaica's wildlife.

A Taste of Paradise: Jamaican Cuisine Unveiled

In the heart of the Caribbean, Jamaica's vibrant and diverse culture extends to its culinary delights, making the island's cuisine a true reflection of its history, people, and bountiful natural resources. Jamaican food is a tantalizing fusion of flavors and influences, enticing food enthusiasts from around the world with its mouthwatering dishes.

One of the most iconic elements of Jamaican cuisine is jerk seasoning. Derived from the Arawak indigenous people, jerk seasoning is a fiery blend of spices, including scotch bonnet peppers, allspice, thyme, and more. This bold and aromatic seasoning is used to marinate and grill meats like chicken, pork, and fish, infusing them with a distinctive smoky flavor that is irresistibly delicious.

No exploration of Jamaican cuisine is complete without a taste of the national dish: ackee and saltfish. Ackee is a fruit native to West Africa and was brought to Jamaica during the days of the transatlantic slave trade. When cooked, ackee bears a striking resemblance to scrambled eggs, making it a unique and flavorful vegan alternative. Combined with salted codfish, onions, tomatoes, and spices, this dish showcases the island's rich cultural heritage and is a beloved staple in Jamaican households.

The influence of the African, European, and Indian heritage is evident in dishes like rice and peas. The dish, featuring coconut milk, kidney beans, and rice, is a testament to the island's diverse ancestry, creating a harmonious blend of flavors that perfectly complements Jamaican main courses.

Seafood plays a prominent role in Jamaican cuisine, given the island's abundance of marine life. Escovitch fish, for example, features fried fish topped with a medley of pickled vegetables and spices, adding a tangy and vibrant twist to the delicate flavors of the fish.

Jamaica's bountiful fruits add a tropical touch to its culinary offerings. The sweet and succulent flavors of mangoes, guavas, pineapples, and papayas are readily available and feature prominently in various desserts, juices, and refreshing beverages.

For those with a sweet tooth, Jamaican desserts are a delightful treat. Coconut drops, made from grated coconut, sugar, and spices, offer a chewy and satisfying indulgence. Additionally, gizzada, also known as "coconut tart," is a pastry filled with a delectable mixture of grated coconut, sugar, and spices, all encased in a buttery crust.

When it comes to beverages, Jamaica is famous for its world-renowned Blue Mountain coffee. Grown in the Blue Mountains, this coffee is known for its smooth and mild flavor, making it a must-try for coffee enthusiasts.

The island's rich volcanic soil also contributes to the thriving agriculture, yielding an abundance of fresh produce like yams, plantains, dasheen, and more. These versatile ingredients are used in a multitude of savory and sweet dishes, showcasing the ingenuity and resourcefulness of Jamaican cooks.

Hospitality is an integral part of Jamaican culture, and nowhere is this more evident than in its traditional Sunday dinners. Families gather together to share a sumptuous meal, featuring a medley of dishes that reflect the warmth and love of Jamaican hospitality.

Jamaican cuisine is more than just food; it is a celebration of flavors, history, and traditions. Whether you're savoring the spicy heat of jerk chicken or relishing the comforting flavors of a hearty bowl of soup, every bite of Jamaican food carries with it a taste of paradise, inviting you to experience the soulful essence of this enchanting Caribbean nation.

Ackee and Saltfish: The National Dish and Beyond

In the heart of Jamaica's culinary tapestry lies a dish that embodies the essence of the island's heritage and flavors: ackee and saltfish. This iconic dish, affectionately known as Jamaica's national dish, is a true celebration of the island's history, culture, and natural bounty.

The story of ackee and saltfish traces back to Jamaica's complex past. Ackee, the star ingredient of the dish, is a fruit native to West Africa and was brought to Jamaica during the days of the transatlantic slave trade. The fruit found a hospitable home in the island's tropical climate and soon became an essential part of Jamaican cuisine.

Today, ackee is not only cherished for its unique taste and texture but also revered for its cultural significance. Ackee's vibrant red pods, when ripe, open to reveal glossy black seeds nestled in a creamy yellow fruit. The fruit itself is a visual delight, reflecting the vivid colors of the Jamaican landscape.

Pairing ackee with salted codfish may seem like an unusual combination, but it is a culinary masterpiece that highlights the fusion of flavors from Jamaica's diverse heritage. The use of salted codfish in Jamaican cooking dates back to the time when European explorers sailed the Caribbean seas. The practice of salting fish was a method of preserving seafood during long sea voyages, and this tradition soon found its way into Jamaican kitchens.

The preparation of ackee and saltfish is an art that requires expertise and finesse. The salted codfish is soaked to remove excess salt, then boiled until tender. The ackee, on the other hand, is carefully prepared to remove any traces of toxins, making it safe for consumption. The cooked ackee is then sautéed with onions, peppers, tomatoes, and various spices, creating a flavorful medley of textures and aromas.

Beyond its status as the national dish, ackee and saltfish holds a special place in the hearts of Jamaicans. It is more than just a meal; it is a symbol of tradition, family gatherings, and the cherished memories shared over Sunday dinners and special occasions.

Ackee and saltfish has also made its mark beyond Jamaica's shores, captivating the palates of food enthusiasts around the world. Jamaican diaspora communities have spread this delectable dish to various corners of the globe, introducing others to the enchanting flavors of the island.

While ackee and saltfish remains at the core of Jamaican cuisine, its versatility shines through in various regional interpretations. In some parts of Jamaica, it is served as a breakfast delight, accompanied by boiled green bananas or fried dumplings. In others, it is enjoyed as a hearty main course for lunch or dinner.

The flavors of ackee and saltfish are as dynamic as the island's ever-changing culinary landscape. Jamaican chefs and cooks continue to explore creative twists and combinations, adding their personal touches to this cherished dish.

Jamaican Jerk: A Fiery Culinary Delight

When it comes to tantalizing the taste buds, Jamaican jerk takes center stage as a fiery culinary delight that leaves an unforgettable impression on those fortunate enough to savor its bold flavors. Originating from the Arawak indigenous people and influenced by the Maroons, jerk seasoning is a mouthwatering fusion of spices, herbs, and scorching scotch bonnet peppers.

The heart of Jamaican jerk lies in its complex and aromatic blend of spices. The key ingredients include allspice (also known as pimento), which adds a warm, slightly sweet note, and scotch bonnet peppers, responsible for the jerk's signature heat. These small but mighty peppers pack a punch and are one of the hottest chili varieties on the Scoville scale. Their vibrant colors, ranging from yellow to red, give the jerk seasoning its fiery flair.

To create the perfect jerk marinade, additional spices like thyme, garlic, ginger, cinnamon, nutmeg, and cloves are combined to form a harmonious blend that complements the intensity of the scotch bonnet peppers. The seasoning is further enriched with the addition of salt and black pepper, enhancing the overall taste experience.

The traditional method of preparing jerk involves marinating meat, typically chicken, pork, or fish, in the jerk seasoning. The meat is then slow-cooked over a pimento wood fire, which imparts a distinct smoky flavor, elevating the dish to new heights. The slow cooking process allows the flavors to meld, infusing the meat with the aromatic goodness of the jerk seasoning.

Jamaican jerk has evolved from humble beginnings to become a global sensation. The irresistible combination of heat, spices, and smokiness has captivated food enthusiasts far beyond Jamaica's shores. From food trucks to high-end restaurants, jerk-infused dishes have made their mark on international menus, thrilling taste buds around the world.

The enchanting flavors of jerk can be experienced in a variety of dishes, each adding its own unique twist to this culinary masterpiece. Jerk chicken, with its tender and succulent meat, is perhaps the most well-known incarnation of this beloved cuisine. The aromatic jerk seasoning permeates the chicken, resulting in a dish that is both spicy and savory, offering a true taste of Jamaica.

Jerk pork is another popular choice, featuring juicy and flavorful cuts of meat that have been slow-cooked to perfection. The mouthwatering jerk seasoning forms a delectable crust on the pork, sealing in the juices and infusing every bite with an explosion of flavors.

For seafood lovers, jerk fish is a delightful option, where the jerk seasoning enhances the natural sweetness of the fish while adding a zesty kick that delights the palate.

Jamaican jerk is not limited to meat and seafood alone. Jerk tofu, a vegan alternative, has gained popularity among those seeking a plant-based version of this fiery delight. The smoky, spicy notes of jerk seasoning complement the tofu, creating a dish that is both satisfying and full of flavor.

While jerk seasoning has become an integral part of Jamaica's culinary identity, the secret to an authentic jerk experience lies in the pimento wood used for cooking. The indigenous pimento tree, also known as the allspice tree, lends its aromatic wood to the fire, infusing the meat with its distinct essence. This element of authenticity is cherished by locals and adds a touch of magic to the overall culinary experience.

In Jamaica, jerk is not just a meal; it's a social event. The tantalizing aroma of jerk permeates the air at bustling jerk centers and roadside stalls, drawing people together to share in the flavors and camaraderie that accompany this beloved culinary tradition.

Jamaican jerk is a testament to the island's rich cultural heritage and the creativity of its people. It embodies the spirit of Jamaica, inviting all who taste it to experience the warmth, vibrancy, and boldness that define this enchanting Caribbean nation. Whether enjoyed on the island itself or savored in far-flung corners of the world, Jamaican jerk is a culinary journey that never fails to leave a lasting impression, forever etching the unforgettable taste of Jamaica in the hearts of all who savor its fiery delight.

Satisfying Your Sweet Tooth: Jamaican Desserts

In the enchanting world of Jamaican cuisine, the indulgence doesn't end with savory delights. Jamaican desserts offer a delectable array of treats that are sure to satisfy any sweet tooth with their delightful flavors and cultural significance.

One of the most beloved Jamaican desserts is coconut drops. These delightful confections are made from grated coconut, sugar, and spices, resulting in a chewy and coconut-infused treat that is a delight for coconut lovers.

Another popular dessert is gizzada, also known as "coconut tart." Gizzadas are small pastries with a buttery crust filled with a delectable mixture of grated coconut, sugar, and spices. These tarts showcase the culinary artistry of Jamaican bakers, combining the richness of butter and coconut with the sweetness of sugar.

Sweet potato pudding is a true taste of Jamaican comfort. Made from grated sweet potatoes, coconut milk, spices, and sugar, this dessert is baked to perfection, offering a moist and flavorful treat that warms the heart and satisfies the palate.

Jamaican fruit cake, known locally as "black cake," is a staple during festive occasions like Christmas and weddings. This dense and flavorful cake is packed with dried fruits, soaked in rum and wine, and spiced with nutmeg and cinnamon. The preparation of black cake often involves a labor of love, as families and friends come together to make the cake, allowing the flavors to mature over time.

The sweet flavors of Jamaica's abundant tropical fruits find their way into a variety of desserts. Pineapple upside-down cake, with its juicy pineapple slices and caramelized brown sugar topping, is a delightful twist on a classic dessert. Fresh mangoes are often enjoyed as a sweet and refreshing treat on their own or transformed into mouthwatering mango sorbet.

For those craving a cool and creamy dessert, soursop ice cream is a must-try. Soursop, a tropical fruit with a custard-like texture and a slightly tangy flavor, is transformed into a luscious ice cream that is both refreshing and exotic.

No discussion of Jamaican desserts would be complete without mentioning the beloved banana fritters. Ripe bananas are mashed and mixed with flour, sugar, and spices, then deep-fried to golden perfection. These fritters are a favorite among locals and visitors alike, offering a delightful balance of sweetness and warmth.

Jamaica's rich dessert offerings are not just a feast for the taste buds; they are a reflection of the island's vibrant cultural heritage. These sweet treats are a part of festive celebrations, family gatherings, and everyday indulgences, embodying the warmth and joy of Jamaican hospitality.

As with any culinary tradition, Jamaican desserts are not static; they continue to evolve and adapt to modern tastes and influences. Chefs and home cooks alike experiment with new flavor combinations and techniques, infusing traditional desserts with contemporary twists.

The enchanting world of Jamaican desserts is an invitation to explore the flavors and traditions of this captivating Caribbean nation. Each dessert offers a glimpse into the heart and soul of Jamaica, where sweetness, warmth, and a passion for culinary artistry come together to create an unforgettable experience for anyone with a penchant for satisfying their sweet tooth. Whether enjoyed on the island's sandy shores or relished in a faraway land, Jamaican desserts are a journey of indulgence and a celebration of the rich cultural heritage that makes them truly special.

Delving into Jamaican Fruits and Tropical Delicacies

As you step into the lush and vibrant landscapes of Jamaica, you are welcomed into a world of tantalizing tropical delights. The island's bountiful fruits and exotic delicacies showcase the diversity of its natural bounty and the creativity of its culinary traditions.

One of the most iconic and sought-after fruits in Jamaica is the ackee (Blighia sapida). This exotic fruit is not only the star of the national dish, ackee and saltfish, but also a beloved ingredient in various other dishes. When ripe, the ackee's bright red pods reveal creamy yellow fruit, which, when cooked, has a texture reminiscent of scrambled eggs. Though ackee is a culinary delight, it must be prepared with care, as consuming it unripe or incorrectly can lead to toxicity.

Mangoes (Mangifera indica) reign supreme among the tropical fruits of Jamaica. The island boasts an array of mango varieties, each with its own unique flavor profile and sweetness. From the juicy East Indian and Bombay varieties to the creamy Julie and the fiberless Tommy Atkins, mango season in Jamaica is a time of celebration.

Soursop (Annona muricata), also known as guanabana, is another highly prized tropical fruit in Jamaica. This large and green fruit has a prickly exterior that conceals a soft and creamy white flesh. Soursop's flavor is a delightful balance of sweetness and tanginess, making it a popular ingredient for juices, desserts, and even ice cream.

Jamaica's pineapple (Ananas comosus) is a succulent treat that is as sweet as it is refreshing. The island's pineapple farms produce a bounty of this tropical fruit, which is a favorite among both locals and visitors. Whether enjoyed fresh, as a tropical garnish, or transformed into tantalizing pineapple upside-down cake, this fruit adds a burst of sunshine to any dish.

Papaya (Carica papaya) is a staple on the Jamaican breakfast table. The vibrant orange flesh of this fruit is both nutritious and delicious, offering a sweet and slightly musky flavor. Served on its own, in fruit salads, or as a garnish for savory dishes, papaya is a versatile and welcome addition to any meal.

The custard apple, or sweetsop (Annona squamosa), is a lesser-known delicacy in Jamaica but a true delight for those who discover it. The fruit's soft and creamy flesh is a heavenly combination of sweetness and a hint of tartness, making it a unique and unforgettable tropical treat.

Jamaica is also home to the unique and flavorful guinep (Melicoccus bijugatus). This small, green fruit is encased in a tough skin that must be cracked open to reveal the juicy pulp inside. Guinep's flavor is both sweet and tangy, and the act of peeling the fruit adds an element of fun to the dining experience.

As you explore Jamaica's culinary offerings, you'll likely encounter various tropical delicacies, each adding its own flair to the island's vibrant food scene. Sweet potato pudding, made from grated sweet potatoes, coconut milk, and spices, is a heartwarming dessert that embodies the comforting essence of Jamaica's traditional recipes.

The Jamaican fruit cake, also known as black cake, is a must-have during festive occasions. This rich and moist cake is loaded with dried fruits, soaked in rum and wine, and spiced with nutmeg and cinnamon. Black cake preparation often involves family traditions and gatherings, where loved ones come together to create this cherished delicacy.

Beyond the fresh fruits and decadent desserts, Jamaica's tropical landscape offers other delights, such as the refreshing coconut water found inside the young coconuts (Cocos nucifera). Sipping coconut water straight from the source is not only a delicious experience but also a refreshing way to quench your thirst on a sunny day.

Jamaica's rich bounty of fruits and tropical delicacies is a testament to the island's abundant natural resources and the creativity of its culinary traditions. Each bite of these tropical delights is a celebration of Jamaica's vibrant culture and the warm hospitality of its people. Whether you're enjoying fresh fruits under the shade of a palm tree or indulging in mouthwatering desserts at a local eatery, delving into Jamaican fruits and tropical delicacies is a journey of taste and discovery, inviting you to experience the true essence of the island's enchanting flavors.

Exploring Jamaica's Iconic Tourist Sights

Jamaica, the gem of the Caribbean, beckons travelers from far and wide with its picturesque landscapes and captivating cultural heritage. From the stunning beaches that grace its shores to the lush mountains that dominate its interior, Jamaica offers a wealth of iconic tourist sights that leave visitors in awe.

One of the most famous sights in Jamaica is Dunn's River Falls, a natural wonder located in Ocho Rios. This magnificent waterfall cascades over terraced limestone rocks, creating a series of breathtaking cascades and pools. Visitors can climb the falls, hand in hand with guides, forming a human chain that allows them to conquer the impressive heights of the cascading waters. The experience is both exhilarating and refreshing, making it a must-do adventure for anyone visiting the island.

The mesmerizing beauty of Negril's Seven Mile Beach is another sight that captivates the hearts of travelers. With its soft, powdery sand and crystal-clear waters, this beach is a postcard-perfect paradise. As the sun sets over the horizon, the beach comes alive with vibrant beach parties and live music, making it a favorite spot for relaxation and entertainment.

For history enthusiasts, a visit to the historic town of Falmouth is a journey back in time. Falmouth boasts a rich architectural heritage, with well-preserved Georgian-style buildings lining its streets. The town's heritage district is a treasure trove of history, offering a glimpse into Jamaica's colonial past and the impact of the sugar industry on the island's development.

In the heart of Jamaica's Blue Mountains lies a haven for coffee connoisseurs: the Blue Mountain Coffee Plantations. Here, visitors can immerse themselves in the lush surroundings of coffee plantations, where the world-renowned Blue Mountain coffee is cultivated. The cool climate and fertile soil of the mountains create the ideal conditions for producing this smooth and flavorful coffee. A visit to the plantations offers a unique opportunity to learn about the coffee-making process, from bean to cup, and savor the aromatic richness of this globally acclaimed coffee.

Ocho Rios is also home to another of Jamaica's iconic tourist sights: Mystic Mountain. This eco-adventure park offers a host of thrilling activities for nature enthusiasts and adventure seekers alike. The Sky Explorer chairlift takes visitors on a scenic journey through the rainforest canopy, offering panoramic views of the surrounding landscapes. For the adrenaline junkies, the bobsled ride down the mountain offers a heart-pounding experience, while the zip line canopy tour allows guests to soar through the treetops with breathtaking views of the Caribbean Sea.

Jamaica's cultural heritage comes alive at the Bob Marley Museum in Kingston, the former home of the reggae legend. The museum offers a glimpse into the life and legacy of Bob Marley, showcasing personal memorabilia, music, and artifacts that celebrate his immense impact on Jamaican and global culture.

For nature lovers, a visit to the Blue Hole in Ocho Rios is a must. This hidden gem is a series of natural pools and waterfalls tucked away in the rainforest. Surrounded by lush greenery and fed by mineral-rich spring water, the Blue Hole offers a refreshing and rejuvenating experience. Adventurous travelers can cliff jump into the crystal-clear waters or swing from ropes, while those seeking tranquility can simply bask in the beauty of nature.

Jamaica's iconic tourist sights extend beyond its shores to the ocean depths. The island is a diving and snorkeling paradise, with abundant marine life and coral reefs waiting to be explored. Locations like Montego Bay Marine Park and the waters off Negril offer excellent opportunities for underwater adventures, where divers can encounter vibrant coral formations, tropical fish, and even the occasional sea turtle or stingray.

Negril's White Sands and Turquoise Waters

Nestled on the western coast of Jamaica, the picturesque town of Negril awaits travelers with its white sands and turquoise waters, creating a paradise that feels like a dream come true. Known for its laid-back vibe and stunning natural beauty, Negril has become a sought-after destination for those seeking an escape to a tropical haven.

The highlight of Negril's allure is undoubtedly its beaches, and Seven Mile Beach takes center stage as a crown jewel of the Caribbean. Stretching along the coast, this pristine beach boasts seven miles of soft, powdery sand that invites visitors to bask under the warm Jamaican sun. The crystal-clear turquoise waters lap gently against the shore, creating a mesmerizing blend of colors that soothe the soul and awaken the senses.

As the sun begins its descent, the Negril sunset becomes a spectacle that must not be missed. Locals and tourists alike gather on the beach to witness the breathtaking sunset that paints the sky with vibrant hues of orange, pink, and purple. This daily ritual is a time of reflection and appreciation, as the horizon transforms into a canvas of nature's artistic brilliance.

For those who seek adventure and adrenaline, Negril's cliff jumping is a thrilling experience. At Rick's Café, daredevils and thrill-seekers leap from the cliffs into the crystal-clear waters below, showcasing their courage as onlookers cheer on with excitement. The adrenaline rush is complemented by the mesmerizing views of the Caribbean Sea and the rugged cliffs that define Negril's landscape.

Beyond the exhilarating cliffs and sandy shores, Negril offers a wealth of water activities that allow visitors to immerse themselves in the beauty of the ocean. Snorkeling is a popular choice, allowing exploration of the vibrant coral reefs and the diverse marine life that inhabits these underwater wonderlands. Schools of colorful fish, graceful rays, and curious sea turtles can be encountered, creating unforgettable encounters with nature.

Negril's laid-back atmosphere is further amplified by its charming beach bars and restaurants. Known for their refreshing cocktails and mouthwatering seafood dishes, these beachside establishments offer a taste of Jamaica's culinary delights, all accompanied by the soothing sounds of reggae music in the background.

For those seeking a more secluded experience, Negril's West End offers a serene escape from the crowds. This rugged and less developed part of Negril is home to boutique hotels, private villas, and quaint guesthouses, offering a peaceful retreat amidst lush greenery and rocky cliffs.

The allure of Negril's white sands and turquoise waters extends beyond its beaches. The nearby Mayfield Falls, a hidden gem, provides an enchanting escape into the heart of nature. This eco-tourist attraction boasts a series of cascading waterfalls and natural pools, offering a refreshing and rejuvenating experience amidst the tropical rainforest.

Negril's charming allure and natural beauty have made it a beloved destination for travelers from all walks of life. Whether seeking adventure, relaxation, or a chance to connect with nature, Negril's white sands and turquoise waters offer an idyllic escape that lingers in the heart and beckons visitors to return time and time again. This Caribbean gem captures the essence of Jamaican hospitality and the splendor of the island's natural wonders, creating an unforgettable experience that leaves a lasting impression on all who venture to its shores.

Ocho Rios: Waterfalls and Beyond

The crown jewel of Ocho Rios is undoubtedly Dunn's River Falls, a breathtaking cascade of terraced limestone rocks that descends into refreshing pools below. This iconic waterfall is a must-visit attraction, allowing visitors to climb the falls hand in hand with guides, forming a human chain that conquers the cascading waters. The experience is both thrilling and invigorating, making it a memory to cherish forever.

For a different waterfall adventure, head to Blue Hole (also known as Secret Falls), a hidden gem tucked away in the rainforest. This secluded oasis offers a series of natural pools and waterfalls surrounded by lush greenery. Visitors can jump from cliffs into the crystal-clear waters, swing from ropes, or simply bask in the tranquility of this enchanting paradise.

Ocho Rios is not just about waterfalls; its stunning beaches are equally enticing. Turtle Beach is a favorite among locals and visitors, with its soft sands and gentle waves perfect for swimming and sunbathing. For those seeking a livelier beach experience, Mahogany Beach offers water sports and beachside bars, creating a vibrant atmosphere for fun and relaxation.

The beauty of Ocho Rios extends beyond its natural wonders to its rich cultural heritage. A visit to the historic town of Falmouth, just a short drive away, reveals well-preserved Georgian-style architecture and a glimpse into Jamaica's colonial past. This heritage district is a testament to the island's history and the legacy of the sugar industry that shaped its development.

The enchanting Green Grotto Caves, located near Ocho Rios, provide an intriguing journey into Jamaica's geological wonders. These limestone caves house fascinating stalactites and stalagmites, creating an otherworldly atmosphere that sparks the imagination. The caves have served various purposes throughout history, from hiding places for Spanish settlers to settings for Hollywood movies.

No visit to Ocho Rios would be complete without experiencing the authentic flavors of Jamaica. The town's local markets and restaurants offer a feast for the senses, with jerk chicken, mouthwatering seafood, and tropical fruits that burst with flavor.

Ocho Rios is a culinary adventure that tantalizes taste buds and celebrates the island's vibrant food culture.

For a memorable day trip, venture to the nearby Rio Grande Valley for a river rafting adventure. Bamboo rafts, guided by skilled captains, glide along the tranquil river, offering a serene journey through lush rainforest scenery. This relaxing excursion is a chance to immerse in nature and witness the untouched beauty of Jamaica's interior.

Ocho Rios' offerings are not limited to its natural beauty and cultural heritage. The town's bustling craft markets are a shopper's paradise, filled with handmade crafts, artwork, and souvenirs that showcase Jamaica's artistic talents and creativity.

The Majesty of the Blue Mountains

As the sun rises over Jamaica, the majestic Blue Mountains cast their spell on all who behold them. Stretching along the eastern edge of the island, these towering peaks are a testament to the breathtaking beauty of nature and the allure of Jamaica's diverse landscapes.

The Blue Mountains are a haven for nature enthusiasts and adventure seekers alike. At an elevation of over 7,400 feet (2,256 meters), they are the highest mountains in Jamaica, shrouded in mist and surrounded by lush rainforests. The cool climate of the mountains provides a refreshing escape from the coastal heat, making it a popular destination for those seeking respite from the tropical sun.

One of the most renowned attractions in the Blue Mountains is the world-famous Blue Mountain coffee. The fertile volcanic soil and unique microclimate of the mountains create the perfect conditions for growing this sought-after coffee variety. The Arabica coffee beans cultivated here are carefully handpicked, sun-dried, and roasted to produce a smooth, aromatic, and flavorful brew that is cherished by coffee connoisseurs around the globe.

The Blue Mountains offer an array of hiking trails that cater to various skill levels, allowing visitors to explore the pristine beauty of the region. Guided hikes take you through lush forests filled with diverse flora and fauna, providing glimpses of endemic bird species like the Jamaican swallow and the ring-tailed pigeon. The trails lead to breathtaking viewpoints, offering panoramic vistas of the island's coastline and the Caribbean Sea, making every step a rewarding and unforgettable experience.

For those seeking a more adventurous challenge, a hike to the summit of Blue Mountain Peak is a true test of determination and stamina. Rising to an elevation of 7,402 feet (2,256 meters), reaching the peak requires an early morning start to catch the sunrise, rewarding hikers with a panoramic view that stretches as far as the eye can see.

Beyond hiking, the Blue Mountains offer an abundance of opportunities for eco-tourism and sustainable practices. Many locals in the region actively participate in eco-friendly initiatives, promoting conservation and responsible tourism to preserve the natural wonders for future generations.

The Blue Mountains' allure extends beyond their natural beauty to the rich cultural heritage of the Maroons, the descendants of escaped slaves who sought refuge in the mountains during the colonial era. The Maroons have preserved their traditions and cultural practices, contributing to the vibrant tapestry of Jamaican culture. Visiting Maroon communities allows travelers to learn about their history, music, dance, and unique way of life.

The Blue Mountains are not just a destination; they are an experience that connects visitors with nature's grandeur and the soul of Jamaica. The breathtaking scenery, the soothing serenity, and the spirit of adventure combine to create an unforgettable journey of discovery and wonder.

The Enigmatic Luminous Lagoon: Nature's Light Show

In the enchanting waters of Jamaica lies a natural wonder that captivates all who witness its magical glow—the Luminous Lagoon. This mysterious body of water, also known as Glistening Waters, is a bioluminescent bay that sparkles with ethereal light, creating a captivating light show that leaves visitors in awe.

Located in Falmouth, on the northern coast of Jamaica, the Luminous Lagoon is one of only a few places in the world where this natural phenomenon occurs. The lagoon is home to microscopic organisms called dinoflagellates, specifically the species Pyrodinium bahamense. These tiny organisms emit a bright blue-green light when they are agitated, creating a mesmerizing display of bioluminescence.

As darkness falls, the Luminous Lagoon comes alive with its otherworldly glow. The movement of the water, whether from boats, fish, or even the human touch, triggers the bioluminescence, turning the lagoon into a sea of shimmering lights. Swirling trails of light follow every movement, creating a surreal and almost magical experience.

One of the most thrilling aspects of visiting the Luminous Lagoon is taking a guided boat tour. As the boat glides through the dark waters, the wake behind it is transformed into a glowing trail of light, an enchanting spectacle that mesmerizes visitors. Some tour operators even encourage visitors to take a dip in the lagoon, allowing them to witness the bioluminescence up close and personal as their bodies create a radiant glow.

The luminous phenomenon in the lagoon is best observed on clear, moonless nights when the darkness allows the bioluminescence to shine brightly. When the moon is full, its light can overpower the glow, making the experience less vivid. Therefore, timing your visit during a new moon phase enhances the luminous effect and offers the most breathtaking display.

Scientists have studied the Luminous Lagoon's unique ecosystem, marveling at the delicate balance that sustains the bioluminescent organisms. The lagoon's shallow and warm waters, combined with the right salinity and nutrient levels, create the ideal conditions for the dinoflagellates to thrive. While the lagoon is a fascinating natural wonder, it is also a fragile ecosystem that requires conservation efforts to preserve its beauty and ensure its longevity.

Beyond its mesmerizing glow, the Luminous Lagoon holds cultural significance for the local community. Jamaican folklore tells tales of the lagoon being haunted by spirits and mythical creatures, adding to the enigmatic allure of this natural wonder. The lagoon's mysterious reputation has made it a subject of intrigue and fascination for generations.

The Luminous Lagoon has become a popular tourist attraction, drawing visitors from around the world who seek to experience the awe-inspiring light show for themselves. Tourists, scientists, and nature enthusiasts alike find themselves captivated by the luminescent magic that unfolds in this secluded bay.

A visit to the Luminous Lagoon is not just a chance to witness nature's light show—it is a journey into the mysteries of the natural world. It is a reminder of the wonders that lie beneath the surface of our planet and the interconnectedness of all living things. As visitors gaze in wonder at the glowing waters, they are reminded of the magic and beauty that surrounds us and are left with a profound appreciation for the marvels of nature that continue to inspire and amaze.

Kingston: The Capital of Culture and Heritage

As the capital city of the island, Kingston is a melting pot of traditions, a center for creativity, and a repository of the nation's rich past. Steeped in history, Kingston's roots date back to the 17th century when it was founded by the English colonists. Over the centuries, the city has evolved, witnessing the rise and fall of empires and becoming a symbol of Jamaica's resilience and determination.

Today, Kingston stands as a cultural powerhouse, offering a myriad of attractions that celebrate the island's identity and artistic legacy. The city's museums, galleries, and performance spaces showcase the creativity and talent of Jamaican artists, writers, musicians, and performers, many of whom have gained global recognition.

The National Gallery of Jamaica, located in Kingston, is the country's premier art institution, housing an extensive collection of Jamaican art from the colonial period to contemporary times. The gallery's exhibits provide a window into the nation's artistic journey, reflecting its history, struggles, and triumphs through visual expressions.

Bob Marley, the legendary reggae icon, is an integral part of Kingston's cultural heritage. The Bob Marley Museum, located at the musician's former residence, pays tribute to his life, music, and profound impact on Jamaican and global culture. Fans and admirers from around the world visit this iconic site to connect with the spirit of the reggae legend and understand the roots of the reggae music movement.

Kingston's music scene extends beyond Bob Marley's legacy, with reggae, dancehall, and ska filling the airwaves and dancehalls throughout the city. The music culture in Kingston is not just about entertainment; it is a reflection of the island's identity, offering a powerful medium for expressing the joys and struggles of life in Jamaica.

For history enthusiasts, the city's architecture tells the story of its colonial past and the struggles for freedom. The historic district of Port Royal, once known as the "wickedest city on Earth," was a notorious pirate haven during the 17th century. Today, it is a

UNESCO-designated heritage site, with ruins and artifacts that provide a glimpse into its colorful and tumultuous history.

Kingston's heritage is also celebrated through its culinary traditions. The city's vibrant food scene offers a fusion of flavors influenced by African, European, and Asian cultures. Local markets, such as the Coronation Market, are a feast for the senses, showcasing a diverse array of fresh produce, spices, and culinary delights that reflect the island's multicultural heritage.

Beyond its cultural richness, Kingston is also a hub for education, commerce, and government. The city houses the University of the West Indies, the region's premier institution of higher learning, nurturing the next generation of leaders, scholars, and innovators.

While Kingston boasts a dynamic urban landscape, it is also surrounded by breathtaking natural beauty. The Blue Mountains provide a stunning backdrop, reminding residents and visitors alike of the harmony between nature and urban life.

Kingston's spirit is a reflection of Jamaica's resilience, creativity, and pride in its heritage. The city is a celebration of life, a testament to the island's journey of progress and self-discovery.

Montego Bay: Jamaica's Gateway to the World

Nestled on the northwest coast of Jamaica lies Montego Bay, a vibrant city that serves as the island's gateway to the world. Known for its picturesque beaches, bustling streets, and warm hospitality, Montego Bay offers a kaleidoscope of experiences that enchant travelers from every corner of the globe.

The history of Montego Bay dates back to the early 16th century when Spanish explorers first set foot on its shores. The city's name "Montego" is derived from the Spanish term "manteca," meaning lard, owing to the abundance of wild pigs in the region during the Spanish colonial era.

Today, Montego Bay is a bustling hub of commerce, tourism, and culture. The city's Sangster International Airport is the busiest airport in Jamaica, welcoming millions of visitors each year from across the Americas, Europe, and beyond. With its extensive flight connections, Montego Bay has become a crucial entry point for tourists eager to experience the wonders of Jamaica.

One of Montego Bay's crown jewels is Doctor's Cave Beach, a pristine stretch of white sand and crystal-clear waters. The beach has a fascinating history, as it was once believed that the water had curative properties due to the presence of minerals. Today, the beach remains a beloved spot for both locals and tourists seeking sun, sea, and relaxation.

The Hip Strip, also known as Gloucester Avenue, is the heartbeat of Montego Bay's tourism and entertainment scene. Lined with restaurants, bars, shops, and clubs, the Hip Strip comes alive after dark with the sounds of reggae music and the laughter of revelers enjoying the vibrant nightlife.

Montego Bay is also home to several championship golf courses, attracting golf enthusiasts from around the world. The city has hosted prestigious golf tournaments, further solidifying its reputation as a world-class destination for both leisure and competitive sports.

For history and architecture buffs, a visit to the Rose Hall Great House is a must. This grand mansion, once owned by the infamous Annie Palmer, known as the "White Witch," is steeped in legends and ghost stories. Tours of the Rose Hall Great House offer a glimpse into Jamaica's colonial past and the captivating lore that surrounds this historic site.

Beyond its urban charm, Montego Bay is surrounded by natural beauty. The Martha Brae River, located just a short drive away, offers a peaceful and scenic river rafting experience. Visitors can glide along the tranquil waters on bamboo rafts guided by expert rafts-men, immersing themselves in the lush greenery and serenity of the Jamaican countryside.

The nearby Montego Bay Marine Park is a haven for snorkeling and diving enthusiasts. The marine park is home to vibrant coral reefs and a diverse array of marine life, including colorful fish, sea turtles, and even the occasional dolphin sighting.

For a taste of Jamaica's cultural heritage, the Montego Bay Cultural Centre provides an immersive experience. The center showcases the island's art, history, and music, paying homage to the nation's rich and diverse heritage.

Montego Bay's allure is not just limited to its shores; it extends beyond the city limits to the stunning landscapes of the surrounding regions. The Cockpit Country, a rugged and untouched limestone forest, is a UNESCO designated biosphere reserve, offering a glimpse into the island's unique biodiversity and geological wonders.

Port Antonio: A Hidden Gem in the Caribbean

As you set foot on the eastern coast of Jamaica, you'll discover a hidden gem that promises an unforgettable escape—Port Antonio. Tucked away from the hustle and bustle of the island's more popular tourist destinations, Port Antonio is a serene and picturesque haven that has earned its reputation as one of the Caribbean's best-kept secrets.

Port Antonio's allure lies in its unspoiled beauty and tranquil ambiance. The town's origins can be traced back to the 16th century when it served as a bustling port for banana exports and trade. Over the years, it has evolved into a serene and charming destination that has captured the hearts of travelers seeking a more laid-back and authentic Caribbean experience.

Port Antonio's beaches are a true reflection of its untouched charm. Frenchman's Cove, with its clear turquoise waters and surrounding lush foliage, exudes a sense of untouched paradise. Its unique location, where a freshwater stream flows into the sea, creates a serene swimming experience that perfectly blends the best of both worlds.

Another treasure awaits at San San Beach, a crescent-shaped cove fringed by palm trees and crystal-clear waters. The beach's calm and shallow waters make it ideal for families and those seeking a leisurely dip in the Caribbean Sea.

The Blue Lagoon is perhaps one of Port Antonio's most iconic attractions. This iridescent, spring-fed lagoon is renowned for its ever-changing shades of blue, ranging from turquoise to cobalt, creating a magical and surreal sight. The lagoon's depth remains a mystery, adding to its enigmatic allure.

For nature enthusiasts, the Rio Grande River provides an adventure like no other. Bamboo rafting along the gentle current of the river offers a serene and scenic experience through lush rainforests and quaint villages, allowing visitors to immerse themselves in the beauty of nature.

Port Antonio's lush landscape extends to the Rio Grande Valley, a paradise for hikers and explorers. The surrounding Blue Mountains create a stunning backdrop, with trails leading to hidden waterfalls and breathtaking viewpoints that offer vistas of the Caribbean Sea and the verdant valleys below.

As a testament to Port Antonio's allure, Hollywood has not been immune to its enchantment. The town and its surroundings have served as the backdrop for several blockbuster movies and music videos, showcasing the natural beauty and captivating charm of this hidden gem.

Port Antonio's intimate size contributes to its charm. The town's warm and welcoming atmosphere is evident in the genuine smiles and friendly greetings of its residents. Visitors often find themselves welcomed like old friends and immersed in the vibrant local culture.

The town's vibrant markets, such as the Port Antonio Craft Market, offer a chance to engage with local artisans and purchase authentic Jamaican crafts and souvenirs. The market's colorful displays and lively atmosphere add to the vibrant spirit of Port Antonio.

Port Antonio's culinary scene celebrates the island's flavors with a focus on fresh and locally sourced ingredients. Seafood lovers will delight in the abundance of freshly caught fish and seafood dishes that grace the menus of the town's restaurants.

Port Antonio's charm lies not only in its natural beauty but also in its ability to offer an authentic and serene escape from the ordinary. It beckons those seeking an unspoiled paradise, where time slows down, and the beauty of nature takes center stage.

Spanish Town: Tracing Jamaica's Colonial Past

As you venture into the heart of Jamaica, you'll find yourself stepping back in time to an era of colonial intrigue and historical significance in Spanish Town. Once the capital of Jamaica during the Spanish and British colonial periods, this city carries the weight of centuries of history, providing a fascinating glimpse into the island's past.

Spanish Town's roots trace back to 1534 when the Spanish established it as their capital, naming it "Villa de la Vega." During their rule, the city thrived as a major center of trade and administration. However, in 1655, the British seized control of Jamaica, and Spanish Town transformed into the capital of the British colony, a position it held until 1872 when Kingston took over as the new capital.

One of the city's most iconic landmarks is the Spanish Town Cathedral, officially known as the St. Catherine of Alexandria Cathedral. This awe-inspiring structure stands as a testament to the city's rich ecclesiastical heritage, with its origins dating back to the 17th century. The cathedral's imposing façade and elegant interior showcase a blend of architectural styles, reflecting the city's colonial past.

The Spanish Town Courthouse is another historic gem that harks back to the city's colonial era. Built in the early 18th century, the courthouse is a fine example of Georgian architecture, characterized by its stately columns and graceful design. It played a crucial role in the island's legal affairs and witnessed many significant historical events.

Beyond its architectural heritage, Spanish Town boasts several museums and heritage sites that offer a deeper understanding of Jamaica's colonial history. The Museum of St. Catherine showcases artifacts and exhibits that highlight the region's social, cultural, and economic development over the centuries.

The nearby Emancipation Square is a poignant reminder of Jamaica's journey toward freedom. This historic square was once the location of a slave market during the dark days of the transatlantic slave trade. Today, it stands as a symbol of emancipation, where the Emancipation Monument pays tribute to the heroes and heroines who fought for freedom and justice.

For those intrigued by Jamaica's military history, the Fort Haldane Ruins provide an intriguing glimpse into the island's past. This former military outpost was built during the 18th century and played a pivotal role in safeguarding the island from potential invasions.

Spanish Town's cultural heritage is also reflected in its vibrant festivals and traditions. The annual St. Catherine Agricultural and Industrial Show is a celebration of the island's agricultural prowess, showcasing a diverse array of produce and livestock, as well as local crafts and products.

Visiting Spanish Town is like stepping into a living history book, where each street and building holds a tale of the past. The city's charming ambiance, combined with its historical significance, creates an immersive experience that transports visitors back in time.

As you walk through the cobblestone streets and admire the historic landmarks, you'll feel the echoes of Jamaica's colonial past reverberate through the present. Spanish Town stands as a testament to the island's resilience, a living testament to the triumphs and struggles that have shaped Jamaica's identity over the centuries.

The city's importance as a center of power and administration during the colonial era has left an indelible mark on the nation's history and culture. Spanish Town's allure lies not only in its historical significance but also in its ability to evoke a sense of nostalgia and reverence for Jamaica's journey toward independence and nationhood.

Spanish Town is a treasure trove of stories and memories, inviting all who visit to become time travelers, exploring the past while appreciating the present. As you delve into Jamaica's colonial past in Spanish Town, you'll find yourself on a voyage of discovery and appreciation for the legacy that lives on in the heart and soul of the nation.

Falmouth: A Historic Georgian Gem

Welcome to Falmouth, a charming town on the northern coast of Jamaica that exudes elegance and heritage with its well-preserved Georgian architecture. Stepping into Falmouth is like stepping into a time capsule that takes you back to the 18th and 19th centuries, where grandeur and refinement were the hallmarks of the era.

Falmouth's history dates back to the late 18th century when it was established by English colonists as a port city for the lucrative sugar trade. Named after the then-governor of Jamaica, Sir William Trelawny, who had family ties to Falmouth, England, the town quickly grew into a bustling center of commerce and culture.

The Georgian architecture in Falmouth is a sight to behold. The town's layout follows a grid pattern, a characteristic of the Georgian style, with elegant streets lined by well-preserved colonial buildings. The facades of these structures feature ornate detailing, including intricate moldings, decorative ironwork, and elegant porticoes, evoking a sense of sophistication and grace.

Falmouth's heritage as a prominent port city is reflected in its historic wharf, which was once a bustling hub of trade and activity. Today, the Falmouth Pier serves as a popular cruise ship terminal, welcoming visitors from around the world to experience the town's historic charm and cultural riches.

The town's centerpiece is Water Square, a charming open space surrounded by historic buildings that served as the hub of social and commercial life in colonial times. Today, the square remains a focal point of Falmouth, hosting events, markets, and celebrations that bring the community together.

Falmouth boasts several well-preserved historic churches, each an architectural marvel in its own right. St. Peter's Anglican Church, a prominent landmark, showcases the neo-Gothic style and boasts beautiful stained-glass windows that add to its splendor.

A walk through the streets of Falmouth is a journey through time, where history and culture intersect. Many of the town's historic buildings have been lovingly restored and repurposed into charming shops, galleries, and restaurants, inviting visitors to immerse themselves in the town's heritage while enjoying modern-day delights.

Beyond its architectural treasures, Falmouth has a vibrant cultural scene that celebrates the island's arts and traditions. The town's annual Trelawny Yam Festival is a lively affair that showcases Jamaica's agricultural heritage and pays homage to the versatile and cherished yam.

The Greenwood Great House, located just outside Falmouth, offers a glimpse into the lives of Jamaica's plantation owners during the colonial era. This well-preserved plantation house is a fine example of the opulent lifestyle enjoyed by the island's elite during that period.

Falmouth's allure as a historic gem extends to its surroundings. The nearby Martha Brae River, known for its gentle rafting experiences, allows visitors to unwind and soak in the natural beauty of the Jamaican countryside.

The town's significance in Jamaica's history has not gone unnoticed, and Falmouth has been designated a National Heritage Site by the Jamaican National Heritage Trust. Efforts to preserve its architectural treasures and cultural heritage have made Falmouth a living testament to the island's colonial past.

A visit to Falmouth is a step back in time to a world of elegance and refinement, where history comes alive through its well-preserved buildings and charming streets. The town's unique blend of heritage and modernity creates an immersive experience that leaves visitors with a profound appreciation for Jamaica's storied past and the people who have shaped its destiny.

The Vibrant Rastafarian Culture of Jamaica

In the heart of Jamaica beats a vibrant cultural movement that has captured the imagination of the world—the Rastafarian culture. Born out of the island's history of struggle and emancipation, Rastafarianism is more than just a religious or social movement; it is a way of life that celebrates freedom, unity, and spiritual enlightenment.

The roots of Rastafarianism can be traced back to the early 20th century, emerging in Jamaica during a time of social and political upheaval. The movement's origins are intertwined with the legacy of Marcus Garvey, a Jamaican activist and advocate for black empowerment. Garvey's teachings emphasized the importance of racial pride, self-reliance, and the return of black people to Africa, their ancestral homeland.

One of the central figures in the early Rastafarian movement was Leonard Howell, also known as "The Gong." Howell's teachings combined elements of Garvey's philosophy with elements of Christianity and African spirituality, creating a unique belief system that resonated with many Jamaicans, especially those from marginalized communities.

The Rastafarian movement gained momentum in the 1930s with the coronation of Emperor Haile Selassie I of Ethiopia. Rastafarians believe that Haile Selassie is the reincarnation of Jesus Christ and the fulfillment of biblical prophecies. He is referred to as "Jah" or "Jah Rastafari," and his coronation marked a significant event in Rastafarian history.

One of the most recognizable symbols of Rastafarian culture is the dreadlocks hairstyle. Rastafarians grow their hair into dreadlocks as a way of embracing their African roots and expressing their commitment to the principles of the movement. The hairstyle also represents a form of resistance against societal norms and a rejection of Western standards of beauty.

Music plays a crucial role in Rastafarian culture, with reggae music acting as the movement's anthem and voice. Reggae artists like Bob Marley, Peter Tosh, and Burning Spear brought Rastafarian beliefs to the forefront of global consciousness through their music. The lyrics of reggae songs often carry messages of social justice, love, and spiritual awakening.

The colors of the Ethiopian flag, green, gold, and red, are symbolic in Rastafarian culture. These colors represent the lush vegetation of Ethiopia, the wealth of the African continent, and the bloodshed of those who fought for liberation and freedom. Rastafarians often wear clothing and accessories adorned with these colors as a visual expression of their identity and beliefs.

Rastafarian culture places a strong emphasis on natural living and a plant-based diet. Many Rastafarians follow a vegetarian or vegan lifestyle, avoiding the consumption of meat and processed foods. The Ital diet, as it is known, is considered to promote physical health and spiritual purity.

Spirituality is at the core of Rastafarian culture, with meditation and prayer playing vital roles in the daily lives of adherents. The Nyabinghi Order is a prominent group within Rastafarianism, known for their gatherings featuring chanting, drumming, and dancing to honor Jah and seek spiritual guidance.

Rastafarian culture's impact reaches far beyond the shores of Jamaica. The movement has inspired individuals worldwide and has been embraced by people of various backgrounds and cultures who resonate with its messages of love, unity, and social justice.

Despite facing challenges and misconceptions over the years, Rastafarian culture remains a vibrant and influential force in Jamaica and beyond. It continues to evolve, adapting to the changing times while staying true to its core principles.

Reggae Music: Bob Marley's Legacy and Beyond

In the colorful tapestry of Jamaican culture, one genre stands out as a symbol of freedom, love, and social consciousness—reggae music. And at the heart of this genre lies the iconic figure whose legacy remains etched in the annals of music history—Bob Marley.

Born in 1945 in Nine Mile, Jamaica, Bob Marley's musical journey began at an early age. With a passion for music and a deep connection to his Rastafarian faith, Marley started performing with childhood friends Peter Tosh and Bunny Wailer, forming the foundation of the iconic reggae group, The Wailers.

In the late 1960s, The Wailers caught the attention of record producer Lee "Scratch" Perry, who played a significant role in shaping their early sound. The group's collaboration with Perry resulted in timeless classics like "Soul Rebel" and "Small Axe," which laid the groundwork for their later success.

In the early 1970s, The Wailers signed with Island Records and released their breakthrough album, "Catch a Fire," in 1973. The album's fusion of reggae with rock elements garnered international acclaim and introduced Bob Marley's music to a global audience.

Bob Marley's lyrics were a powerful reflection of the social and political issues of his time. Songs like "Get Up, Stand Up" and "Redemption Song" became anthems of resistance and hope, inspiring people worldwide to stand up against oppression and fight for justice.

It was in 1977 that Bob Marley released what would become one of the most influential albums in music history—"Exodus." The album's title track, along with songs like "Jamming" and "One Love," solidified Marley's status as a reggae icon and brought reggae music to the forefront of the international music scene.

Beyond his musical talent, Bob Marley's life was a testament to his unwavering commitment to love and unity. His tireless advocacy for peace and his vision of a world without prejudice touched the hearts of millions, transcending cultural and geographical boundaries.

Tragically, Bob Marley's life was cut short when he passed away at the age of 36 in 1981 after battling cancer. However, his spirit lives on through his music, which continues to inspire generations of artists and listeners alike.

In the wake of Marley's passing, the reggae movement he championed continued to evolve. Artists like Peter Tosh, Bunny Wailer, and Jimmy Cliff carried the torch, keeping reggae's flame alive while also infusing it with their unique styles and perspectives.

Reggae music's influence has spread far beyond Jamaica's shores. The genre's uplifting rhythms and heartfelt lyrics resonated with people around the world, leading to the emergence of reggae scenes in places as far-reaching as the United Kingdom, Africa, and the United States.

In the 1990s, the reggae-rock fusion genre gained popularity, with bands like Sublime and 311 blending elements of reggae, ska, and punk to create a fresh and distinct sound.

Today, reggae music continues to thrive, with contemporary artists like Damian Marley, Chronixx, and Protoje carrying the mantle of their predecessors, infusing their music with social commentary and messages of love and unity.

Bob Marley's legacy is indelible. His music, message, and spirit remain a guiding light for those who seek a better world and a more harmonious existence. He is a symbol of the power of music to transcend barriers and unite people, making reggae not just a genre of music, but a movement of love and liberation.

Dancehall: The Rhythmic Heartbeat of Jamaica

If reggae music is the soul of Jamaica, then dancehall is its rhythmic heartbeat—a genre that has taken the world by storm with its infectious beats, clever wordplay, and unapologetic expression of Jamaican culture. Originating in the late 1970s, dancehall has since become a global phenomenon, drawing fans from all corners of the globe.

Dancehall's roots can be traced back to the sound systems of Kingston, Jamaica. These sound systems, mobile DJ setups with massive speakers, played a crucial role in shaping the genre. They brought music to the streets, playing the latest reggae and dancehall tunes to captivated audiences.

Early dancehall artists, like Yellowman, Shabba Ranks, and Sister Nancy, paved the way for the genre's success with their innovative style and bold lyrics. Dancehall's energetic rhythms and catchy melodies quickly captivated listeners, making it a mainstay in Jamaica's music scene.

The dancehall culture extends far beyond just the music. Dancehall dances and fashion have become an integral part of Jamaican identity. The dance moves, known for their high energy and acrobatic flair, are a way for people to express themselves and let loose on the dance floor.

The fashion associated with dancehall is also distinctive, with artists and fans alike embracing vibrant colors, bold prints, and streetwear influences. Dancehall fashion reflects the genre's rebellious spirit, allowing individuals to make a statement and showcase their unique style.

One of the defining features of dancehall is its emphasis on freestyle lyricism and wordplay. Artists engage in "clashes," where they compete in impromptu battles of wit and skill, often incorporating playful insults and clever rhymes. These clashes are not just about competition; they are a celebration of lyrical prowess and creativity.

In the 1990s, dancehall took on an international dimension, spreading its influence beyond the shores of Jamaica. Artists like Sean Paul and Shaggy achieved worldwide success, introducing dancehall to new audiences and solidifying its place in mainstream music.

The dancehall movement also brought with it the concept of "riddims." A riddim is a distinctive instrumental track that various artists can record their own songs over, creating a compilation of tunes on a single rhythm. This practice became a hallmark of the genre, allowing artists to showcase their unique styles while riding the same infectious beat.

Dancehall's impact on global pop culture cannot be overstated. From dancehall-inspired fashion trends to dance moves that have become viral sensations, the genre's influence is felt across various artistic disciplines.

As dancehall continues to evolve, new generations of artists are pushing the boundaries of the genre, incorporating elements of hip-hop, afrobeats, and other musical styles. Dancehall remains a dynamic and ever-evolving genre, capturing the essence of Jamaica's vibrant spirit.

However, dancehall has not been without its controversies. Some critics have raised concerns about explicit lyrics and violent themes present in some dancehall songs. Others argue that these songs are a reflection of the harsh realities faced by many Jamaicans and serve as a platform for social commentary.

Despite the controversies, dancehall remains an essential part of Jamaican culture, an outlet for expression, and a driving force in the island's creative landscape. Its rhythmic heartbeat resonates with fans worldwide, creating a sense of unity and celebration of Jamaican identity.

Junkanoo: A Festive Celebration of African Roots

In the vibrant tapestry of Jamaican culture, there is one celebration that stands out as a colorful and rhythmic ode to the island's African heritage—Junkanoo. This festive extravaganza is a time-honored tradition that brings communities together, fostering a sense of unity and pride in Jamaica's rich cultural legacy.

The origins of Junkanoo can be traced back to the days of slavery when African slaves on the island were granted brief periods of freedom during the Christmas holidays. These precious moments of respite allowed them to gather and express their cultural identity through music, dance, and costumes.

The name "Junkanoo" is believed to have evolved from the West African word "John Canoe," which referred to a West African king who was renowned for his generosity and benevolence. Over time, the celebration took on various influences, including those from the indigenous Taino people and European settlers, creating a unique and distinct Jamaican tradition.

The heart of Junkanoo lies in its lively parades and vibrant displays of music and dance. Each year, on Boxing Day (December 26th) and New Year's Day, communities across Jamaica come alive with the sounds of drums, cowbells, whistles, and horns, as revelers take to the streets in elaborate costumes and masks.

The making of Junkanoo costumes is a labor of love that takes months of preparation. Intricate designs, adorned with feathers, sequins, and bright colors, transform participants into walking works of art. The costumes are a testament to the creativity and craftsmanship of the Jamaican people.

The music of Junkanoo is equally captivating, featuring a cacophony of traditional instruments, including goatskin drums, conch shells, and homemade wind instruments. The infectious rhythms and melodies are impossible to resist, drawing spectators into the festivities and encouraging them to dance along.

Junkanoo parades are not just a spectacle for the eyes and ears; they are a reflection of Jamaican identity and pride. Participants come together as a community, displaying a sense of unity and belonging that transcends differences and celebrates the shared heritage of African roots.

Beyond its significance in Jamaica, Junkanoo also has a presence in other parts of the Caribbean, most notably in the Bahamas, where it is an integral part of the country's cultural fabric. In the Bahamas, Junkanoo takes place on Boxing Day and New Year's Day, just like in Jamaica, but with its own unique twists and interpretations.

In recent years, efforts have been made to preserve and promote the tradition of Junkanoo, with various organizations and events dedicated to showcasing this cultural treasure. The Jamaica Cultural Development Commission (JCDC) plays a crucial role in preserving and promoting the island's cultural heritage, including Junkanoo.

The popularity of Junkanoo has also extended beyond the Caribbean, with people around the world embracing the celebration and incorporating elements of it into their own festivities and events.

Junkanoo serves as a living reminder of Jamaica's African heritage, an embodiment of the resilience and creativity of its people. It is a celebration of freedom and identity, a testament to the enduring spirit that flows through the veins of the nation.

Embracing the Laid-Back Lifestyle of Jamaica

Jamaica's laid-back vibe is evident from the moment you set foot on the island. The warm smiles of the locals, the rhythmic beats of reggae music, and the tranquil landscapes all contribute to an atmosphere of serenity and ease.

The concept of "Jamaican time" perfectly encapsulates the laid-back lifestyle. Clocks and schedules take a backseat to the natural flow of life. It's a place where the phrase "soon come" is an expression of patience and a reminder to savor the present moment.

In Jamaica, the emphasis is on enjoying life, spending time with family and friends, and appreciating the simple pleasures. Whether it's gathering on the beach to watch the sunset, sharing a meal with loved ones, or engaging in spontaneous dance and song, the spirit of togetherness is at the core of the laid-back lifestyle.

The laid-back lifestyle is reflected in the cuisine of Jamaica, too. Jamaican food is a fusion of flavors influenced by African, European, and indigenous Taino traditions. The island's signature dishes, such as jerk chicken, ackee and saltfish, and coconut-infused delights, are a celebration of simplicity and natural ingredients.

One of the hallmarks of the laid-back lifestyle is the importance of relaxation and unwinding. The idyllic beaches and lush landscapes provide the perfect backdrop for basking in the sun, taking leisurely strolls, or indulging in a refreshing dip in the crystal-clear waters.

Jamaica's laid-back spirit extends beyond the beach towns and into the heart of its bustling cities. In places like Kingston, Montego Bay, and Ocho Rios, you'll find a mix of vibrant energy and an easygoing attitude. The cities offer a blend of cultural experiences, from visiting historic sites to exploring local markets, all with a sense of unhurried joy.

For many Jamaicans, spirituality and faith play a significant role in embracing the laid-back lifestyle. The island's Rastafarian culture, in particular, embodies a philosophy of peace, love, and unity, encouraging individuals to find harmony within themselves and with the world around them.

Jamaica's landscape itself seems to embody the essence of the laid-back lifestyle. The Blue Mountains, with their misty peaks and lush coffee plantations, exude tranquility and an air of contemplation. The cascading waterfalls and hidden lagoons offer an escape into nature's calming embrace.

Laid-back living also extends to the way Jamaicans celebrate, with festivals and gatherings that highlight the island's rich cultural heritage. Events like Junkanoo, Reggae Sumfest, and the Accompong Maroon Festival are occasions to revel in music, dance, and the joy of being together.

As you immerse yourself in the laid-back lifestyle of Jamaica, you'll discover that it's not just about taking it easy—it's about being present in every moment, savoring the connections with others, and finding a sense of contentment and balance within yourself.

In Jamaica, the laid-back lifestyle is not a fleeting trend; it's an ingrained part of the island's soul, woven into the fabric of its identity. It's a reminder that sometimes the most meaningful experiences in life come from embracing the simplicity of being and finding joy in the little things.

So, whether you're lounging on the beach, sipping a freshly blended fruit drink, or swaying to the rhythm of reggae music, remember to embrace the laid-back lifestyle of Jamaica—a gift that invites you to slow down, breathe, and truly appreciate the beauty of life.

Festivals and Celebrations: Joyous Jamaican Traditions

Jamaica is a land of vibrant colors, infectious rhythms, and a rich tapestry of traditions, all of which come to life through its festivals and celebrations. From lively street parades to solemn religious observances, these joyous occasions are a reflection of the island's culture, history, and spirit.

One of the most iconic and beloved festivals in Jamaica is the annual Reggae Sumfest. Held in Montego Bay, this music extravaganza celebrates the island's renowned reggae genre. For several days, locals and visitors alike come together to revel in the sounds of their favorite reggae artists, with performances that light up the night and create an atmosphere of pure joy and unity.

Another notable festival is the Accompong Maroon Festival, a unique celebration of the island's Maroon heritage. Taking place in January in the remote hills of St. Elizabeth Parish, this festival honors the brave Maroon warriors who fought for their freedom during the era of slavery. Visitors have the chance to immerse themselves in Maroon culture, enjoying traditional music, dance, and food while learning about the history and traditions that define this resilient community.

In February, Jamaica comes alive with vibrant colors and spirited celebrations during the annual carnival, known as Bacchanal Jamaica. This carnival is a spectacle of masquerade bands, music, dancing, and a vibrant display of costumes adorned with feathers, sequins, and glitter. The streets of Kingston and other major cities become a carnival of revelry, as participants and spectators alike embrace the festive spirit with gusto.

For a unique and traditional celebration, the Jonkonnu Festival takes center stage during the Christmas season. With roots dating back to the days of slavery, this festival is a mix of African, European, and indigenous traditions. Dressed in colorful costumes, performers known as "Jonkonnu dancers" dance through the streets, blending music, dance, and theatrical performances in a joyous display of cultural heritage.

As Easter approaches, Jamaicans take part in an age-old tradition known as "Bun and Cheese." Families and friends come together to enjoy this delectable combination of spiced bun and creamy cheese, symbolizing the end of Lent and the beginning of the Easter festivities.

Religious observances are an integral part of Jamaica's cultural calendar, and one of the most significant is the celebration of Emancipation Day on August 1st. On this day, Jamaicans commemorate the abolition of slavery in the British colonies. The day is marked with solemn ceremonies, cultural performances, and educational events that honor the sacrifices and struggles of their ancestors.

In addition to these traditional festivals, Jamaica also observes various religious holidays, including Christmas and Easter, with a unique Jamaican twist. The Christmas season is particularly special, with a festive atmosphere, street parties, and the joyful sound of Christmas carols blending with reggae renditions of classic holiday tunes.

Throughout the year, Jamaicans celebrate the joy of life and the blessings of their culture through a myriad of local and community-based events. These gatherings provide an opportunity for everyone to come together, share their talents, and honor the spirit of unity that defines Jamaican identity.

The Influence of Religion in Jamaican Culture

Religion plays a significant role in shaping the cultural landscape of Jamaica. From the moment you set foot on the island, you'll encounter a diverse array of religious practices, each contributing to the rich tapestry of Jamaican culture. Throughout history, religion has been a unifying force, bringing communities together and providing a source of hope, comfort, and guidance.

One of the most prominent religions in Jamaica is Christianity, with the majority of Jamaicans identifying as Christians. The two largest denominations are Protestantism, including various branches like Baptist, Anglican, Methodist, and Pentecostal, and Roman Catholicism. These Christian traditions have deep roots in Jamaican society, dating back to the days of European colonization.

Protestantism, in particular, has a significant influence on Jamaican culture and spirituality. Many churches play an active role in their communities, providing not only a place of worship but also educational, social, and humanitarian services. The Christian faith is often woven into the fabric of everyday life, shaping moral values, family dynamics, and social interactions.

Beyond Christianity, another major religious influence in Jamaica is the Rastafari movement. Founded in the 1930s, the Rastafari movement emerged as a response to the social and political injustices faced by Jamaicans, particularly those of African descent. Rastafarians believe in the divinity of Emperor Haile Selassie I of Ethiopia, whom they see as the earthly manifestation of God, and embrace a way of life centered around peace, love, and equality.

The Rastafari movement's impact on Jamaican culture extends beyond its religious beliefs. Rastafarian culture has contributed significantly to Jamaican music, with reggae legends like Bob Marley and Peter Tosh being prominent Rastafarian figures. Reggae music, with its messages of peace, unity, and social consciousness, is deeply intertwined with the Rastafari philosophy and has become a global symbol of Jamaican identity.

The Rastafari movement also influenced Jamaican art, literature, and fashion. Rastafarian colors, such as red, green, gold, and black, are often featured in artistic expressions, clothing, and accessories, representing the movement's core values.

Judaism, Islam, Hinduism, and other religious beliefs also find representation in Jamaica, reflecting the country's diverse and multicultural society. These religious traditions have carved out spaces for worship and community, contributing to the rich tapestry of Jamaican religious life.

In addition to organized religions, Jamaicans also maintain a strong connection to their ancestral spiritual practices. Obeah and Myal are traditional Afro-Jamaican belief systems that incorporate elements of African spirituality, herbal medicine, and ritual practices. These belief systems, while not as prominent as organized religions, continue to play a role in shaping Jamaican cultural identity and belief systems.

Religious celebrations and observances are an essential part of Jamaican culture. From Christmas to Easter, Diwali to Eid, religious holidays are marked with special rituals, feasts, and gatherings, bringing families and communities together in celebration and reflection.

The influence of religion is not limited to sacred spaces. Jamaican culture is characterized by its spiritual expressions in everyday life. You'll often hear Jamaicans expressing gratitude to God or saying a prayer before a meal. Religious references are also woven into daily conversations, songs, and even colloquial expressions.

Religion in Jamaica is not just about beliefs; it is a way of life—a guiding force that shapes morals, values, and interactions with others. It provides a sense of community, a source of strength during challenging times, and a celebration of the joys of life.

Art and Craftsmanship: Expressions of Jamaican Creativity

In the heart of Jamaica, a vibrant and dynamic arts scene thrives, expressing the island's soul and creativity in a myriad of forms. From colorful paintings to intricate sculptures, and from handmade crafts to elaborate performances, Jamaican art and craftsmanship are a celebration of the island's cultural richness and creative spirit.

One of the most prominent artistic expressions in Jamaica is its visual art. The island boasts a talented community of painters, sculptors, and mixed-media artists whose works capture the essence of Jamaican life, nature, and culture. Jamaican art often showcases the beauty of the island's landscapes, the vibrancy of its people, and the warmth of its spirit.

The Jamaican art scene has produced world-renowned talents, such as Barrington Watson, who gained international acclaim for his captivating portraits and landscapes. Other notable artists include Mallica "Kapo" Reynolds, who created stunning sculptures and paintings inspired by his Rastafarian beliefs, and the incomparable Edna Manley, whose pioneering work as a sculptor and advocate for the arts left an indelible mark on Jamaican culture.

Jamaican art also reflects the country's history and social struggles. Artists often use their creations to address issues of identity, social justice, and political activism. Through their art, they give voice to the collective consciousness of the Jamaican people, shining a light on the challenges and triumphs that have shaped their nation.

Craftsmanship in Jamaica is equally captivating, with skilled artisans preserving traditional practices while infusing them with contemporary flair. One such example is the exquisite Jamaican pottery, where artists mold clay into beautiful and functional objects, reflecting the island's natural beauty and cultural motifs.

Wood carving is another hallmark of Jamaican craftsmanship, with artists skillfully shaping wood into intricate sculptures and figurines. These carvings often depict scenes from Jamaican folklore, spirituality, and everyday life, offering a glimpse into the island's rich cultural heritage.

The art of basket weaving is deeply ingrained in Jamaican tradition, passed down through generations. The intricate designs and vibrant colors of these handwoven baskets reflect the creativity and resourcefulness of the Jamaican people.

Jamaican craftsmanship is also celebrated in the realm of music and dance. Traditional music instruments, such as the marimba, bongo drums, and the bamboo flute, are lovingly crafted by skilled hands, ensuring that the island's musical traditions continue to thrive.

In the realm of performance arts, Jamaica's vibrant dance culture is a testament to the island's artistic prowess. From the rhythmic moves of traditional folk dance, like the Jonkonnu and Kumina, to the electrifying energy of dancehall and reggae routines, Jamaican dancers captivate audiences with their skill and passion.

Art festivals and cultural events are essential showcases for Jamaican creativity. The Jamaica Biennial, held by the National Gallery of Jamaica, is a prominent event that celebrates contemporary visual art, providing a platform for emerging artists to showcase their talents and perspectives.

Jamaican art and craftsmanship are not confined to galleries and museums; they are woven into the very fabric of Jamaican life. They are present in the vibrant murals adorning city walls, in the exuberant costumes of street performers, and in the everyday objects that exude a touch of artistic flair.

The importance of art in Jamaican culture extends beyond aesthetics; it is a means of storytelling, of preserving traditions, and of celebrating the unique identity of the Jamaican people. Art and craftsmanship are expressions of the island's soul—a testament to its creativity, resilience, and unwavering spirit.

Literature and Poetry: The Written Soul of Jamaica

In the literary world, Jamaica shines as a beacon of creativity and expression, with its rich literary traditions giving voice to the island's soul and spirit. Jamaican literature and poetry are a celebration of the country's cultural diversity, historical legacy, and the resilience of its people.

The written word has long held a special place in Jamaican culture. From the early days of colonization to the present, Jamaican authors and poets have used their craft to capture the essence of their nation, weaving tales of triumph and tribulation, love and loss, and the triumph of the human spirit.

One of the most iconic figures in Jamaican literature is Louise Bennett-Coverley, affectionately known as "Miss Lou." Her poetry and prose in Jamaican Patois (Creole) celebrated the island's language, customs, and folklore. Miss Lou's works bridged the gap between the written and spoken word, bringing Jamaican culture to life on the page and the stage.

Another literary giant is the prolific Jamaican novelist and playwright, Claude McKay. McKay's poetry and novels, such as "Banjo" and "Home to Harlem," explored themes of race, identity, and the African diaspora, making him a significant voice in the Harlem Renaissance—a movement that celebrated African American culture and creativity.

The influence of Jamaican literature extends to contemporary authors like Marlon James, who gained international acclaim for his novel "A Brief History of Seven Killings." The book, which delves into the political turmoil and music scene of 1970s Jamaica, won the prestigious Man Booker Prize and brought Jamaican literature to a global audience.

Jamaica's literary scene is not limited to prose and poetry; it also encompasses folktales, fables, and oral storytelling passed down through generations. These tales offer insights into the island's history, values, and beliefs, serving as a reminder of the power of storytelling to connect communities and preserve cultural heritage.

Poetry has been a cherished art form in Jamaica, with poets using language as a vehicle to express their thoughts, emotions, and reflections on life. From the soul-stirring verses of Una Marson to the thought-provoking poetry of Lorna Goodison, Jamaican poets have left an indelible mark on the literary world.

Language is a defining aspect of Jamaican literature and poetry. Many writers infuse their works with Jamaican Patois, a vibrant language that reflects the island's diverse heritage and linguistic influences. The use of Patois adds authenticity and intimacy to the storytelling, capturing the unique rhythm and flavor of Jamaican life.

Jamaican literature is also deeply influenced by the island's historical struggles and triumphs. The legacy of slavery and the fight for independence are recurring themes in many works, shedding light on the resilience and spirit of the Jamaican people.

Literary festivals and events, such as the Calabash International Literary Festival, provide platforms for Jamaican and international writers to come together, share their stories, and engage with audiences. These gatherings celebrate the power of literature to transcend borders and connect hearts.

In schools and communities across Jamaica, literature and poetry hold a special place in education and cultural celebrations. Students are exposed to the works of Jamaican authors, fostering an appreciation for their heritage and inspiring the next generation of writers and poets.

Jamaican literature and poetry are not just a reflection of the island's past; they are a testament to its present and future—a powerful vehicle for preserving traditions, documenting history, and celebrating the diverse voices that make up the Jamaican identity.

Patois: The Colorful Language of the Island

In the vibrant tapestry of Jamaican culture, one of the most captivating threads is the language known as Patois. This colorful and expressive dialect, also called Jamaican Creole, is an integral part of the island's identity, reflecting the rich history and diverse influences that have shaped Jamaica's unique linguistic landscape.

Patois is a dynamic fusion of African, English, Spanish, and indigenous languages, with each contributing its distinct flavor to the mix. It emerged during the era of slavery when Africans from different regions were brought to Jamaica and needed to communicate with each other and their European captors.

The roots of Patois can be traced back to West African languages, such as Akan, Igbo, and Yoruba, which were combined with English words and phrases. Over time, as Jamaican society evolved, Patois continued to evolve, absorbing elements from other languages and cultures.

The evolution of Patois is a testament to the resilience and creativity of the Jamaican people. It served as a tool for communication and cultural preservation during a dark chapter in history, helping to forge a collective identity among the enslaved Africans and their descendants.

Patois is not a single unified language but rather a group of related dialects that can vary from region to region and even from one community to another. Despite its informal origins, Patois has earned its place as a vibrant and respected language, spoken and understood by Jamaicans from all walks of life.

One of the unique aspects of Patois is its rhythm and intonation, which give the language a musical quality. The melodic cadence of Patois is often likened to the island's pulsating reggae beats, creating a seamless blend of language and music that embodies the soul of Jamaica.

While English is the official language of Jamaica, Patois is widely spoken in informal settings and is an essential part of everyday communication. It is used in homes, on the streets, in markets, and among friends and family. For many Jamaicans, Patois is not just a means of communication; it is an expression of their cultural pride and heritage.

Over the years, Patois has also found its way into Jamaican literature, music, and art, becoming a source of inspiration for writers, poets, and musicians. In the realm of music, reggae and dancehall artists infuse their lyrics with Patois, creating a distinctive and authentic sound that resonates with audiences worldwide.

Jamaican proverbs and sayings in Patois offer profound insights and wisdom, passed down through generations. These expressions are often peppered with humor and wit, reflecting the resourcefulness and creativity of the Jamaican people.

In recent years, there has been a growing appreciation for Patois as a symbol of national identity and cultural heritage. Efforts have been made to preserve and celebrate the language, with initiatives promoting its use in schools and cultural events.

While Patois is beloved by Jamaicans, it can sometimes be challenging for visitors to fully understand. However, most Jamaicans are gracious and patient with those eager to learn and embrace their language.

In the melting pot of Jamaica's linguistic landscape, Patois stands as a vibrant emblem of the island's multicultural heritage. Its rich history, captivating rhythms, and expressive phrases paint a vivid picture of the Jamaican experience, capturing the essence of the island's soul. Patois is more than just words; it is a celebration of the resilience, creativity, and unity of the Jamaican people—an enduring testament to the power of language to connect hearts and transcend borders.

Jamaican English: Understanding the Linguistic Blend

In the captivating linguistic landscape of Jamaica, a fascinating blend of languages unfolds, resulting in Jamaican English, a unique and expressive form of communication. Jamaican English, often referred to as "Standard Jamaican English" or "Jamaican Standard English," is distinct from Patois but equally significant in shaping the island's cultural identity.

At its core, Jamaican English is a variety of the English language, influenced by historical, social, and cultural factors that have shaped the Jamaican experience. With its roots in British colonialism, English was introduced to Jamaica during the 17th century, serving as the language of administration, education, and trade.

Over time, the English spoken in Jamaica evolved, absorbing elements from various languages, including African, Spanish, and indigenous tongues. This linguistic fusion led to the development of Jamaican English, a vibrant and dynamic form of the language that reflects the diverse heritage of the island.

One of the distinguishing features of Jamaican English is its pronunciation. Jamaicans often employ distinctive intonation and stress patterns, creating a rhythmic and melodious quality to the language. This musicality is reminiscent of the island's rich cultural heritage, with echoes of reggae beats and dancehall rhythms woven into everyday speech.

Vocabulary is another aspect that sets Jamaican English apart. The language is peppered with colorful expressions, idioms, and phrases that reflect the island's unique identity and cultural nuances. Jamaicans are known for their wit and humor, which shines through in their use of language, adding a delightful flair to everyday conversations.

Jamaican English is the language of education and official communication in the country. It is taught in schools and used in formal settings such as government offices, businesses, and the media. While English is the official language, Jamaican English is deeply ingrained in Jamaican society, playing a significant role in shaping national discourse and identity.

In contrast to Patois, Jamaican English is more standardized and follows the rules of grammar and syntax of British English. It serves as a unifying language, connecting Jamaicans from different regions and social backgrounds, allowing for clear and efficient communication in diverse settings.

However, it's important to note that Jamaican English exists on a continuum, with various levels of proficiency and usage. Some Jamaicans may be more comfortable speaking in Patois in informal settings, while using Jamaican English in more formal contexts.

In recent years, there has been a growing appreciation for Jamaican English as an essential aspect of Jamaican culture. Efforts have been made to promote the use of Jamaican English in literature, arts, and media, recognizing its significance in preserving the island's linguistic heritage.

While Jamaican English may sometimes be misunderstood or mistaken for Patois by outsiders, it is an essential part of the island's linguistic landscape. Learning and understanding Jamaican English allow visitors and newcomers to connect with the Jamaican people on a deeper level, appreciating the rich tapestry of language and culture that defines the island.

Exploring Jamaican Folklore and Superstitions

In the enchanting world of Jamaican culture, folklore and superstitions weave a captivating tapestry of myths, legends, and beliefs that reflect the island's rich history and diverse heritage. Jamaican folklore is deeply rooted in the oral tradition, passed down through generations, carrying the wisdom, fears, and dreams of the Jamaican people.

One of the most iconic figures in Jamaican folklore is Anansi, the clever spider. Anansi is a trickster character known for his cunning and wit, often outsmarting other creatures and even gods. His stories, handed down through generations, entertain and teach valuable life lessons.

Another popular folk character is the "duppy," a ghost or spirit said to roam the island. Duppies are believed to be the restless souls of the deceased, and Jamaicans have a rich tradition of ghost stories and encounters. Many claim to have experienced eerie encounters with duppies, leading to the belief in the power of obeah—the practice of using supernatural forces for good or ill.

The tale of the "rolling calf" is another spine-tingling legend in Jamaican folklore. This mythical creature is said to be a large, glowing, one-eyed calf that terrorizes those who encounter it. The story of the rolling calf is often used to caution children against wandering alone at night.

The belief in "duppy houses" is a superstition deeply ingrained in Jamaican culture. Duppies are said to inhabit certain places or objects, such as abandoned houses or old trees, and people often avoid these areas, fearing encounters with restless spirits.

Jamaican folklore is also replete with tales of "Jamaican witches," often referred to as "Jankunu" or "Old Higue." These witches are believed to have the ability to transform into various forms, including animals, and cause harm to others through dark magic. The concept of witches in Jamaican folklore is both feared and respected.

Superstitions play a significant role in Jamaican life, shaping various aspects of daily routines and decision-making. One common superstition involves the belief in "bad luck" if a black cat crosses your path. Many Jamaicans consider it inauspicious to walk under a ladder, and the number "7" is often considered lucky.

The practice of "ring games" is a cherished tradition in Jamaican folklore, where singers and musicians gather to perform traditional songs and dances, often accompanied by folklore characters. Ring games are a celebration of cultural heritage and a way to keep folklore alive.

In rural areas, "Myal" and "Pocomania" are two religious practices deeply rooted in Jamaican folklore. These syncretic religious traditions combine elements of Christianity with African spiritual beliefs and rituals, showcasing the fusion of cultural influences on the island.

Jamaican folklore also includes beliefs related to the natural world. For instance, the sighting of certain animals, such as owls and bats, is often interpreted as omens of impending death or misfortune.

Additionally, the Jamaican tradition of "Nine-Night" ceremonies is a testament to the island's folklore and cultural heritage. These ceremonies are held to honor and remember the deceased, with singing, dancing, and storytelling playing a central role in the celebration.

While many Jamaicans embrace and celebrate their folklore and superstitions, some aspects have been met with skepticism and criticism, especially those associated with dark magic and harm. However, the importance of folklore in preserving cultural identity and passing down traditions cannot be understated.

The Impact of Sports on Jamaican Identity

In the heart of Jamaica beats a passionate love for sports that transcends boundaries and unites the nation. From the sun-kissed beaches to the rugged mountains, sports have woven themselves into the very fabric of Jamaican identity, shaping the island's culture, instilling pride, and leaving an indelible mark on the global stage.

One sport that embodies the spirit of Jamaica is track and field. The island's prowess in athletics is legendary, and Jamaica has produced a plethora of world-class sprinters and long-distance runners. From the iconic Usain Bolt, known as the "fastest man alive," to Shelly-Ann Fraser-Pryce, the "Pocket Rocket," Jamaican athletes have captivated the world with their blazing speed and unyielding determination.

The success of Jamaican track and field athletes on the international stage has not only brought glory to the island but also instilled a sense of national pride. Every victory and record-breaking moment is celebrated with fervor and jubilation, as the entire nation rallies behind its athletes, chanting "Jamaica to the world!"

Sports have become a vehicle for social mobility and empowerment in Jamaica. The success stories of athletes rising from humble beginnings to international acclaim serve as inspiration for young Jamaicans, encouraging them to dream big and pursue their goals with tenacity.

Beyond track and field, cricket holds a special place in Jamaican hearts. Cricket is deeply ingrained in the island's history, and Jamaicans take great pride in their cricketing legacy. The legendary West Indies cricket team, which includes Jamaican cricketing icons like Michael Holding and Courtney Walsh, has brought honor and distinction to the Caribbean region.

In recent years, football (soccer) has also gained popularity in Jamaica. The Reggae Boyz, as the national football team is affectionately known, have been making strides on the international stage, qualifying for the FIFA World Cup in 1998—a significant achievement that further solidified Jamaica's sporting identity.

Sports serve as a unifying force in Jamaica, transcending social, economic, and political divides. Regardless of background or status, Jamaicans come together to celebrate their athletes and teams, forging a shared sense of camaraderie and national pride.

The impact of sports on Jamaican culture extends beyond the realm of competition. Sports have become a means of promoting health and wellness, with numerous community-based initiatives aimed at encouraging physical activity and active lifestyles.

Furthermore, sports play a vital role in fostering discipline, teamwork, and perseverance among young Jamaicans. Sports programs in schools and communities provide a platform for personal growth and development, equipping the youth with essential life skills that extend far beyond the playing field.

Jamaica's sporting achievements have also contributed to the country's reputation as a global powerhouse in athletics. The success of Jamaican athletes has put the island on the map, drawing international attention and admiration for the nation's sporting prowess.

Jamaican sports culture is not limited to elite athletes; it also includes a vibrant network of local and amateur sporting events that engage communities across the island. From inter-school competitions to neighborhood football matches, sports foster a sense of belonging and togetherness among Jamaicans.

The impact of sports on Jamaican identity is evident in the expressions of national pride during major sporting events. The waving of the black, green, and gold flag, the donning of Jamaican-themed attire, and the singing of the national anthem are all symbolic of the deep connection between sports and national identity.

Sports have become a source of hope and inspiration for Jamaica, a nation that has faced its share of challenges and adversity. Whether on the track, the field, or the cricket pitch, Jamaican athletes carry the dreams and aspirations of a nation, embodying the spirit of resilience and determination that defines the Jamaican people.

Jamaica's Love for Cricket and Athletic Glory

In the sun-kissed paradise of Jamaica, a love affair with sports has blossomed, capturing the hearts of its people and becoming an integral part of the island's cultural identity. Among the array of sports that have taken root in Jamaica, two stand out with resounding passion and fervor: cricket and athletics.

Cricket holds a hallowed place in Jamaican history, harkening back to the days of British colonial rule. The lush green cricket grounds and the sound of leather on willow evoke nostalgia for a bygone era. Cricket is more than just a sport; it is a symbol of resilience, camaraderie, and national pride.

The West Indies cricket team, representing several Caribbean nations, has long been an emblem of sporting excellence. Jamaica has been a proud contributor to this prestigious team, producing a legion of cricketing legends who have etched their names into the annals of sporting history.

Among the cricketing luminaries from Jamaica is the iconic Michael Holding, affectionately known as "Whispering Death." Holding's mastery of pace bowling and his fierce competitiveness on the field earned him global acclaim and a revered place in cricketing folklore.

Another towering figure in Jamaican cricket is Courtney Walsh, who held the record for the most Test wickets until surpassed by Muttiah Muralitharan. Walsh's humility and unyielding dedication to the game endeared him to fans worldwide, making him an adored ambassador for the sport.

Jamaica's love affair with cricket extends beyond international competitions. Local cricket clubs and school teams form the bedrock of the sport, nurturing young talents and instilling in them the virtues of discipline, sportsmanship, and teamwork.

In addition to cricket, athletics has become a source of pride and glory for Jamaica. The island's prowess on the track has catapulted it to the forefront of global athletics, showcasing the raw talent and tenacity of its athletes.

Jamaica's love for athletics can be traced back to the early 20th century when Norman Manley, a prominent figure in Jamaican politics and sports, founded the Jamaica Amateur Athletics Association (now the Jamaica Athletics Administrative Association). This laid the foundation for the nation's athletic journey.

However, it was the emergence of "The Boss," Usain Bolt, that brought Jamaica's athletic glory to dazzling heights. Bolt's lightning speed and charismatic personality captivated the world, earning him the title of the "fastest man alive" and turning him into a global sporting icon.

Bolt's unrivaled dominance in sprint events at the Olympics and World Championships showcased Jamaica's prowess on the track. Alongside Bolt, other Jamaican athletes such as Shelly-Ann Fraser-Pryce, Elaine Thompson-Herah, and Yohan Blake have added to the island's legacy of athletic greatness.

The success of Jamaican athletes on the international stage has not only brought glory to the nation but has also inspired the youth of Jamaica to dream big and pursue their sporting passions with zeal. Many aspiring young athletes look to their track and field heroes as role models, emulating their dedication and commitment to excellence.

Athletics has become more than just a sport; it is a vehicle for social mobility and empowerment in Jamaica. Numerous sports programs and initiatives aim to harness the potential of young athletes and provide them with opportunities to succeed both on and off the track.

The love for cricket and athletics runs deep in the veins of every Jamaican. The electric atmosphere in the stands during cricket matches and the thunderous applause that reverberates through the stadiums during athletic events are a testament to the passion and fervor with which Jamaicans embrace sports.

Jamaica's love for cricket and athletics has transformed these sports into unifying forces, bridging divides and creating a sense of national pride. Whether it's the roar of the crowd during a thrilling cricket match or the anticipation of a record-breaking sprint on the track, sports unite the nation in celebration and solidarity.

Healing Traditions: Jamaican Medicinal Practices

Amid the lush landscapes and vibrant culture of Jamaica lies a treasure trove of traditional healing practices that have been passed down through generations. Jamaican medicinal practices are deeply rooted in the island's rich history, blending elements from African, Indigenous, and European traditions to create a unique and holistic approach to healing.

Herbal remedies are at the heart of Jamaican traditional medicine. The island's diverse flora provides a wealth of medicinal plants that have been used for centuries to treat various ailments. Herbs such as aloe vera, ginger, soursop, fever grass (lemongrass), and moringa are just a few examples of the plants valued for their healing properties.

Jamaican herbalists, known as "bush doctors" or "bush teas," are the custodians of this ancient knowledge. These healers possess a deep understanding of the medicinal properties of plants and use their expertise to create herbal concoctions tailored to specific health needs.

One of the key beliefs in Jamaican traditional medicine is the concept of balancing the body's energies. The philosophy is rooted in the idea that illness is caused by an imbalance in the body's natural flow of energies. Herbal remedies and rituals are used to restore harmony and promote healing.

Another essential aspect of Jamaican medicinal practices is the use of rituals and spiritual elements. Many healers believe that spiritual forces play a crucial role in the healing process. Rituals, prayers, and the use of talismans are often employed to invoke divine assistance in the healing journey.

One well-known Jamaican medicinal practice is "baths" or "bush baths." These herbal baths are prepared using a combination of healing plants and are believed to cleanse the body, alleviate pain, and promote overall well-being. Bush baths are an integral part of traditional healing ceremonies.

In addition to herbal remedies, Jamaican traditional medicine also encompasses massage, acupuncture, and bone-setting techniques. These practices are often combined with herbal treatments to provide a holistic approach to healing.

Jamaican medicinal practices are deeply ingrained in the cultural fabric of the island. They are not just a means of treating physical ailments but also a reflection of the Jamaican people's close connection to nature and their belief in the power of the spiritual world.

While modern medicine is widely available in Jamaica, traditional healing practices continue to thrive and are embraced by many as a complementary or alternative form of treatment. The holistic nature of Jamaican medicinal practices, addressing the physical, spiritual, and emotional aspects of health, appeals to those seeking a more comprehensive approach to healing.

The preservation and continuation of Jamaican medicinal practices are upheld by dedicated healers and the communities they serve. These healers pass down their knowledge through apprenticeships, ensuring that the wisdom of traditional medicine is safeguarded for future generations.

It is essential to recognize that traditional healing practices are not without controversy and skepticism. Some question their efficacy and safety, while others emphasize the need for evidence-based medicine. As with any healing modality, it is crucial to exercise caution and seek professional advice when dealing with health concerns.

Nonetheless, Jamaican traditional medicine continues to be a source of comfort and hope for many. Its profound connection to the island's history, culture, and spirituality makes it an integral part of Jamaica's identity.

In exploring the healing traditions of Jamaica, one gains insight into the resilience, resourcefulness, and profound wisdom of the Jamaican people. The herbal remedies, rituals, and practices are a testament to the enduring power of traditional knowledge and the enduring spirit of healing that continues to thrive in the heart of Jamaica.

Ecotourism in Jamaica: Preserving Paradise

Amidst the azure waters and lush landscapes of Jamaica lies a growing movement that seeks to harmonize tourism with environmental conservation—ecotourism. With its rich biodiversity and stunning natural beauty, Jamaica has emerged as an idyllic destination for travelers seeking to connect with nature while promoting sustainability.

Ecotourism in Jamaica is not just about sightseeing; it is about forging a profound connection with the island's delicate ecosystems and taking active steps to preserve them. From the majestic Blue Mountains to the verdant rainforests and pristine coral reefs, Jamaica offers a diverse array of ecotourism opportunities that captivate the hearts of adventurers and nature enthusiasts alike.

One of the crown jewels of Jamaican ecotourism is the Blue and John Crow Mountains National Park, a UNESCO World Heritage Site. This mountain range is a sanctuary for rare and endangered species, including the Jamaican blackbird and the critically endangered Jamaican iguana. Hiking through these mist-covered mountains allows visitors to immerse themselves in Jamaica's natural wonders while contributing to the preservation of this invaluable ecosystem.

Another ecotourism hotspot in Jamaica is the Cockpit Country, a rugged and biodiverse region known for its unique limestone formations and endemic flora and fauna. Exploring the Cockpit Country provides an opportunity to encounter Jamaica's rich geological and ecological history, as well as support local communities engaged in sustainable tourism practices.

Jamaica's coastal areas are also integral to its ecotourism efforts. The island is blessed with numerous marine protected areas, including the Negril Marine Park and the Montego Bay Marine Park. These protected zones safeguard vibrant coral reefs, seagrass beds, and mangrove forests that serve as vital habitats for a myriad of marine species. Snorkeling and diving in these areas offer a chance to witness the kaleidoscope of marine life while contributing to the preservation of fragile underwater ecosystems.

Ecotourism in Jamaica goes beyond traditional nature-based activities. Community-based tourism initiatives empower local communities to actively participate in sustainable tourism practices. Visitors can engage with rural communities, learn about traditional crafts, savor authentic Jamaican cuisine, and contribute to community-led conservation projects. These interactions create a deeper understanding of Jamaican culture and foster a sense of responsibility towards preserving the environment.

Sustainable accommodations are also gaining traction in Jamaica's ecotourism landscape. Eco-lodges and eco-resorts strive to minimize their environmental impact, employing renewable energy sources, recycling programs, and nature-conscious architecture. Staying at these establishments allows travelers to experience the beauty of Jamaica while treading lightly on the planet.

The economic benefits of ecotourism in Jamaica extend beyond local communities. Revenue generated from sustainable tourism initiatives is reinvested in conservation efforts, education programs, and the protection of natural habitats. This cycle of reinvestment ensures the long-term viability of ecotourism and its positive impact on Jamaica's environment and society.

However, like any form of tourism, ecotourism faces its challenges. Balancing the influx of visitors with environmental protection requires careful planning and regulation. Responsible ecotourism management seeks to control visitor numbers, implement sustainable infrastructure, and establish clear guidelines to minimize ecological disruption.

Jamaica's commitment to ecotourism is exemplified by the Blue Flag program—a prestigious international eco-certification awarded to beaches and marinas that meet stringent environmental criteria. The Blue Flag beaches, such as Frenchman's Cove in Port Antonio, represent Jamaica's dedication to preserving its coastal environments while providing visitors with pristine beach experiences.

As ecotourism gains momentum in Jamaica, it is essential to continue raising awareness about sustainable travel practices among tourists and locals alike. The collective efforts of individuals, businesses, and policymakers play a vital role in protecting Jamaica's natural wonders for generations to come.

Jamaica's Unique Blend of Modern and Traditional Architecture

In the heart of the Caribbean lies Jamaica—a land of vibrant culture, breathtaking landscapes, and a rich architectural tapestry that weaves together the island's past and present. Jamaica's architecture is a fascinating reflection of its history, culture, and the diverse influences that have shaped the nation over the centuries.

One cannot talk about Jamaican architecture without acknowledging the enduring legacy of colonialism. The Spanish and British colonial periods left a profound imprint on the island's built environment. Spanish colonial architecture can still be seen in structures like the historic Spanish Town Cathedral, a UNESCO World Heritage Site and one of the oldest Anglican churches in the Caribbean.

British colonial influence is evident in the majestic Georgian-style buildings that grace cities like Kingston and Falmouth. These grand structures, with their stately facades and ornate detailing, stand as a testament to Jamaica's colonial past and its significance as a hub of trade and commerce.

Amidst the colonial architecture, traditional Jamaican vernacular architecture shines through. The Jamaican "gingerbread houses" are a quintessential example of this style, characterized by intricate wooden fretwork, bright colors, and charming verandas. These houses represent a fusion of African, European, and indigenous influences, creating a unique architectural identity that is unmistakably Jamaican.

The architecture of Jamaica's Great Houses also reflects the island's colonial history. These opulent plantation estates were once the domain of wealthy British landowners, and their grandeur is a stark reminder of the stark social and economic disparities of the past. Today, many of these Great Houses have been repurposed as cultural landmarks and heritage sites, offering visitors a glimpse into Jamaica's complex history.

As Jamaica moved into the 20th century, modernist architecture began to make its mark on the island. The architectural style known as "Jamaican Modern" emerged, characterized by clean lines, simple forms, and a seamless integration with the natural surroundings. The work of renowned Jamaican architect Gordon "Bunny" Steadman exemplifies this style, with projects like the Liguanea Club and the Jamaica Pegasus Hotel showcasing the marriage of modern design and tropical aesthetics.

In recent years, sustainable and eco-friendly architecture has gained momentum in Jamaica. With a growing awareness of environmental issues, architects and designers are incorporating eco-conscious practices into their projects. Sustainable materials, energy-efficient design, and passive cooling techniques are becoming integral to modern Jamaican architecture.

In addition to the influence of colonial and modern styles, Jamaican architecture is deeply rooted in its cultural heritage. The Rastafarian movement, with its focus on natural materials and spiritual connection with the environment, has inspired eco-friendly and eco-spiritual architecture on the island.

The use of bamboo as a sustainable building material has gained popularity in Jamaica, with innovative structures like the Bamboo Cathedral in Portland showcasing the versatility and beauty of this eco-friendly resource.

Jamaica's architectural landscape is also shaped by the needs and aspirations of its people. Informal settlements, known as "yards," are prevalent in urban areas, reflecting the resourcefulness and resilience of the Jamaican people in creating vibrant and close-knit communities.

The architectural diversity of Jamaica is a testament to the island's ability to evolve while preserving its cultural heritage. It is a vibrant tapestry that speaks to the interplay of history, culture, and modernity—a living testament to Jamaica's journey from past to present.

Sustainability and Environmental Challenges in Jamaica

In the enchanting paradise of Jamaica, where turquoise waters meet golden beaches and lush rainforests, the delicate balance between tourism and environmental preservation becomes a pressing concern. While Jamaica's natural beauty is a major draw for tourists, the island faces significant sustainability challenges that demand urgent attention.

One of the foremost environmental issues in Jamaica is deforestation. The island's dense rainforests are home to a vast array of unique flora and fauna, but they are under threat from logging and illegal clearing for agriculture and development. Deforestation not only leads to the loss of valuable biodiversity but also exacerbates soil erosion and contributes to climate change.

Another pressing challenge is the degradation of coastal ecosystems, particularly coral reefs. These fragile marine habitats are vital for the island's tourism industry, as they support diverse marine life and provide snorkeling and diving opportunities for visitors. However, factors like pollution, overfishing, and climate change-induced coral bleaching are posing significant threats to Jamaica's reefs.

Pollution, especially from plastic waste and runoff from agricultural practices, is a growing concern for Jamaica's coastal and marine environments. Plastics not only mar the natural beauty of beaches but also harm marine life, with turtles, fish, and seabirds often falling victim to ingesting or becoming entangled in plastic debris.

Water pollution extends beyond coastal areas, with inland water bodies also facing contamination from agricultural runoff and untreated wastewater discharge. The health of rivers and freshwater resources is critical for both the environment and local communities' well-being, making water pollution a top sustainability challenge.

Climate change is another pressing issue confronting Jamaica. The island is vulnerable to the impacts of rising sea levels, extreme weather events, and changing precipitation patterns. These changes can disrupt agriculture, damage infrastructure, and displace communities, requiring adaptive measures to safeguard the island's future.

As an island nation, Jamaica is also susceptible to the threats posed by rising ocean temperatures. The phenomenon known as coral bleaching, driven by warmer waters, can lead to the mass die-off of coral reefs, further imperiling marine biodiversity and tourism.

Jamaica's biodiversity, though rich, faces significant threats from invasive species. Introduced plant and animal species can outcompete and displace native species, disrupting fragile ecosystems. Efforts are underway to control and manage invasive species, but it remains an ongoing challenge. In response to these environmental challenges, Jamaica has taken steps to promote sustainability and conservation. The establishment of protected areas and marine parks, such as the Blue and John Crow Mountains National Park and the Negril Marine Park, demonstrates the country's commitment to preserving its natural heritage.

Sustainable tourism practices are also gaining momentum in Jamaica. Eco-friendly accommodations, community-based tourism initiatives, and responsible tour operators aim to reduce the industry's impact on the environment while supporting local communities. Efforts are underway to improve waste management and reduce plastic pollution in Jamaica. Public awareness campaigns and initiatives to promote recycling and sustainable waste practices are being implemented to tackle this critical issue.

Jamaica is also investing in renewable energy sources to reduce its carbon footprint. Solar and wind energy projects are being developed to transition towards cleaner energy alternatives.

Environmental NGOs and community-based organizations play a vital role in driving sustainability efforts in Jamaica. They collaborate with the government and local communities to advocate for environmental protection, conservation, and sustainable practices.

Despite these efforts, the challenges facing Jamaica's environment are complex and multifaceted. Collaboration between government, businesses, local communities, and international partners is essential to tackle the root causes of environmental degradation and work towards a more sustainable future for Jamaica.

Jamaican Economy: From Agriculture to Tourism

Jamaica's economic journey is as diverse as its cultural heritage and natural landscapes. From the fertile plains of its agricultural heartland to the sun-kissed shores that beckon tourists from around the globe, the island's economic evolution has been shaped by a myriad of factors.

Historically, agriculture played a pivotal role in Jamaica's economy, dating back to the days of sugar and coffee plantations during the colonial era. The fertile soil and favorable climate made the island an ideal location for cultivating sugarcane, which became a dominant export crop. However, the legacy of plantation-based agriculture also left a complex socio-economic legacy, with the system of slavery and indentured labor shaping the island's social fabric.

While sugarcane and coffee were once the driving forces behind Jamaica's agricultural sector, the industry faced significant challenges over the years. Fluctuating global market prices and the rise of competitors in the international market led to a decline in the profitability of these traditional crops. As a result, Jamaica diversified its agricultural output to include a range of other products, such as bananas, citrus fruits, cocoa, and yams.

In recent times, the service sector, particularly tourism, has emerged as a vital pillar of Jamaica's economy. With its stunning beaches, vibrant culture, and warm hospitality, Jamaica has become one of the most sought-after destinations in the Caribbean for travelers seeking sun, sand, and unique experiences.

Tourism contributes significantly to Jamaica's gross domestic product (GDP) and provides employment opportunities for a large portion of the population. The tourism industry encompasses a wide range of services, from hotels and resorts to tour operators, restaurants, and transportation services. It has spurred the growth of various ancillary industries, supporting local artisans, musicians, and craft markets.

The development of the tourism sector has not been without challenges. Like many island destinations, Jamaica faces competition from other Caribbean nations and must continuously innovate to maintain its appeal to tourists. Additionally, the seasonal nature of tourism can lead to fluctuations in economic activity, necessitating measures to address employment stability and economic resilience.

To further diversify its economy, Jamaica has also sought to attract foreign investment in sectors like manufacturing, information technology, and financial services. The establishment of free trade zones and export-oriented industries has helped stimulate economic growth and create employment opportunities beyond tourism and agriculture.

Despite progress, Jamaica has faced economic challenges and periods of fiscal constraint. High levels of public debt and structural issues within the economy have necessitated efforts to promote fiscal responsibility, attract foreign investment, and improve the business climate.

Efforts to promote small and medium-sized enterprises (SMEs) have also gained traction in Jamaica. These enterprises play a crucial role in fostering entrepreneurship, job creation, and innovation, contributing to the island's economic diversity and resilience.

As Jamaica continues to navigate its economic landscape, sustainability and inclusivity remain key considerations. The pursuit of green initiatives, renewable energy development, and responsible tourism practices all factor into the vision for a more sustainable economic future.

The government of Jamaica, in collaboration with international organizations and development partners, has implemented policies to foster economic growth, alleviate poverty, and strengthen social welfare programs. Education and skills development initiatives aim to equip the workforce with the competencies needed to thrive in a globalized economy.

Education and Literacy in Jamaica

Education and literacy are the foundation of any thriving society, and Jamaica recognizes their pivotal role in shaping the nation's future. The journey towards establishing a robust education system in Jamaica has been a testament to the country's commitment to providing opportunities for its people to excel and prosper.

Formal education in Jamaica has deep historical roots, dating back to the early 18th century when schools were established by religious organizations and colonial authorities. However, access to education was limited, and education opportunities were largely confined to the elite and privileged.

With the dawn of independence in 1962, Jamaica placed education at the forefront of its development agenda. The government sought to make education accessible to all, recognizing it as a powerful tool to break the cycle of poverty and empower individuals to contribute meaningfully to society.

One of the landmark achievements in Jamaica's education history was the introduction of free and compulsory primary education in 1973. This move marked a significant step towards inclusivity, ensuring that children across the island had the opportunity to attend school and receive a basic education.

The government's commitment to education further extended to the establishment of community colleges and technical institutions, offering vocational training and skills development. These initiatives aimed to equip students with practical skills and prepare them for the workforce, contributing to the country's economic growth and development.

Jamaica also recognized the importance of early childhood education in laying a strong foundation for lifelong learning. The Early Childhood Commission was established to regulate and oversee the quality and standards of early childhood institutions, ensuring that children receive a nurturing and stimulating learning environment from a young age.

Literacy rates in Jamaica have shown significant improvement over the years. According to UNESCO, the literacy rate for adults aged 15 years and older was estimated to be around 88% in 2018.

This achievement is a testament to the country's efforts in promoting literacy and expanding access to education for all.

Jamaica has also been proactive in addressing gender disparities in education. The government has worked to ensure equal educational opportunities for both boys and girls, encouraging gender parity in enrollment and academic achievement.

The development of the education system in Jamaica has not been without its challenges. The country has faced issues such as overcrowded classrooms, shortages of qualified teachers, and infrastructural limitations. Efforts are continuously made to address these challenges and enhance the quality of education offered to students.

To promote innovation and adaptability in education, Jamaica has embraced the integration of technology in the learning process. The use of digital resources and e-learning platforms has enabled greater access to educational materials, especially in remote and underserved areas.

Jamaica's commitment to education extends beyond its shores. The country has actively participated in educational initiatives at the regional and international levels, collaborating with organizations such as the Caribbean Examinations Council and participating in international assessments like the Programme for International Student Assessment (PISA).

The future of education in Jamaica holds great promise, with ongoing efforts to improve teacher training, enhance curriculum development, and strengthen the overall education system. Investing in the education of the youth is recognized as a key driver for social and economic progress, and Jamaica remains dedicated to nurturing the talents and potential of its young population.

Social Issues and Challenges Faced by the Nation

Jamaica, like any other nation, grapples with a myriad of social issues and challenges that require thoughtful consideration and collective action. These issues touch the lives of Jamaicans from all walks of life and shape the fabric of society.

One of the most pressing challenges facing Jamaica is poverty and income inequality. While the country has made significant progress in reducing poverty rates over the years, there remains a significant wealth gap between the rich and the poor. Poverty disproportionately affects vulnerable groups, including children, single-parent households, and individuals living in rural areas.

Unemployment is another critical social issue in Jamaica. Despite efforts to promote economic growth and create jobs, the country continues to face high unemployment rates, particularly among young people. Youth unemployment poses a significant concern, as it can lead to disillusionment, social unrest, and a sense of hopelessness among the youth.

Crime and violence have long been pervasive social challenges in Jamaica. The country has grappled with high rates of violent crime, including homicides, gang-related activities, and drug-related offenses. The impact of crime extends beyond immediate victims, affecting communities, businesses, and the overall sense of security in the nation.

In recent years, there have been efforts to address crime and violence through various initiatives, including community-based interventions, crime prevention programs, and targeted law enforcement measures. However, sustained progress requires addressing underlying social factors that contribute to criminal behavior, such as poverty, inequality, and lack of educational opportunities. The issue of education also intersects with social challenges in Jamaica. While significant strides have been made in expanding access to education, the quality of education remains an area of concern. Disparities in educational outcomes persist, with students from disadvantaged backgrounds often facing barriers to achieving academic success. Teenage pregnancy is another social issue that merits attention. Jamaica has one of the highest rates of teenage pregnancy in the Caribbean region, with significant implications for young girls' health, education, and overall well-being. Addressing this challenge requires comprehensive sexual education, access to reproductive healthcare, and efforts to empower young girls and women.

Substance abuse, particularly drug abuse, is an ongoing concern in Jamaica. The availability and use of illicit drugs contribute to a range of social problems, including crime, violence, and health issues. Substance abuse rehabilitation and prevention programs are vital components of addressing this challenge.

Discrimination and social prejudice also persist in Jamaican society. Marginalized groups, including the LGBTQ+ community, face stigmatization and lack legal protections in some areas. Addressing discrimination requires fostering a more inclusive and accepting society that respects the rights and dignity of all individuals.

Housing and homelessness are also significant social issues in Jamaica. Informal settlements, or "squatter communities," exist in urban areas, where residents lack access to basic services and adequate housing. Providing affordable housing and improving living conditions for vulnerable populations remain priorities for the government. Healthcare access is another social challenge faced by the nation. While Jamaica has made progress in improving healthcare services, access remains uneven, particularly in rural areas. Addressing health disparities and ensuring equitable access to healthcare are essential for the well-being of all Jamaicans.

Family structure and dynamics have also evolved over time in Jamaica. Single-parent households are prevalent, and there is a growing number of families headed by women. This shift in family dynamics brings both opportunities and challenges, as it influences child-rearing, economic stability, and support systems.

As Jamaica continues to address these social issues and challenges, it does so with a spirit of resilience, community strength, and commitment to progress. Government policies, civil society initiatives, and individual actions all play a role in shaping a more equitable, inclusive, and thriving Jamaican society.

Epilogue

As we come to the end of this journey through the vibrant tapestry of Jamaica, it's essential to reflect on the captivating story of this Caribbean gem. Jamaica, with its rich history, mesmerizing landscapes, and dynamic culture, has left an indelible mark on the hearts of travelers and locals alike.

The island's history, steeped in the legacies of indigenous communities, European colonization, and the struggles for independence, has shaped the resilient and spirited nature of its people. From the bravery of the Maroons defending their freedom to the triumphs of Jamaican athletes on the global stage, the nation's history is woven with stories of courage and determination.

The enchanting wildlife and exotic cuisine found on the island showcase the biodiversity and natural abundance that Jamaica has to offer. From the majestic Blue Mountains to the mesmerizing Luminous Lagoon, nature's wonders beckon visitors to revel in the island's unspoiled beauty.

Jamaica's cultural heritage, with its colorful festivals, pulsating music, and expressive arts, exemplifies the island's vibrant soul. Reggae music, Bob Marley's enduring legacy, and the rhythmic heartbeat of dancehall all resonate with the world, spreading messages of love, unity, and social consciousness.

Throughout this exploration, we've witnessed the fusion of tradition and modernity, as Jamaica embraces its past while forging ahead into the future. From the quaint towns steeped in colonial architecture to the bustling cities teeming with energy and creativity, the island's architectural blend reflects its unique identity.

Yet, Jamaica also grapples with social challenges, striving to overcome issues such as poverty, crime, and education disparities. The spirit of resilience and community strength shines through, as the nation works collectively to address these challenges and build a more equitable society.

As we bid farewell to the captivating world of Jamaica, let us carry with us the lessons learned from this remarkable nation. Let us cherish the beauty of its landscapes, the warmth of its people, and the richness of its culture. May Jamaica's story inspire us to embrace our own heritage, celebrate diversity, and stand united in the pursuit of a brighter, more inclusive world.

And so, as the sun sets over the turquoise waters of the Caribbean, let the spirit of Jamaica's vibrant soul continue to resonate in our hearts, reminding us that despite our differences, we are all connected, and our stories are intertwined on this beautiful journey of life.

Printed in Great Britain
by Amazon